More Praise for *Change Your Questions, Change Your Life*

"Our complex world demands that we ask different questions, but the power of habit throws us into the Judger Pit. Dr. Adams shows us how to get out of the Judger Pit and stay out—and how to improve our relationships, our work, and our lives with the different questions we ask."
—**Jennifer Garvey Berger, PhD, coauthor of *Simple Habits for Complex Times* with Keith Johnston**

"It's hard to describe *Change Your Questions* without using superlatives such as *life-changing*, *remarkable*, and *mind-opening*. There's a reason this book has been an international bestseller...It has awakened readers to a new model of thinking, a new understanding of collaboration and communication...applicable in all aspects of life...It can uplift not only you, the reader, but everyone around you."
—**G. Shawn Hunter, author of *Out Think* and cofounder and President, MindScaling**

"This groundbreaking work advances not only the way leaders think about leadership and coaching but how they approach life. It has opened doors for thousands of our Key Executive Leadership Program graduates, exposing them to a world of reflection, questioning, and professional and personal growth...transformational in every sense of the word!"
—**Patrick S. Malone, PhD, Director, Key Executive Leadership Programs, Department of Public Administration and Policy, American University**

"Question Thinking has led to a radical transformation in how our teams and leaders approach problems. It also made an immediate and sustained change in their behavior. In an organizational culture, the more that people can be taught these processes, the greater positive impact they can have on productivity and the bottom line."
—**Carmella Granado, Senior Director, Organizational Effectiveness, Flextronics**

"*Change Your Questions* is an easy, fun story with profound and transformational possibilities...elegant, well-designed tools offer practical help for creating lastin̲ ̲ ̲ ̲ ̲aspect of health care."
—**David W. Moen, MD,**

"This insightful approach to business and personal problem-solving is so powerful that it is surely destined to have a major impact in the business world."

—**Kathy Leech, Executive Director, Corporate Brand and Advertising, Comcast**

"A wonderful contribution to the world of Action Learning!"

—**Bea Carson, PhD, cofounder and President, World Institute for Action Learning**

"*Change Your Questions* provides an invaluable road map for helping you truly understand the best way to get to the core of the issues you face. A high-impact read for every human resource and leadership development professional."

—**Steve Miranda, Managing Director, ILR School, Cornell University**

"As a leadership coach and behavioral scientist, I know how essential it is for people to shift mindsets in order to change their behavior and their lives. Dr. Adams provides a simple and brilliant system for opening the mind so breakthroughs can occur."

—**Marcia Reynolds, PsyD, author of *The Discomfort Zone* and Past President, International Coach Federation**

"Question Thinking offers patients, families, and clinicians a new paradigm for patient and relationship-centered care. This simple yet profound framework has the potential to transform health care."

—**Cynda Hylton Rushton, PhD, RN, FAAN, Anne and George L. Bunting Professor of Clinical Ethics, Berman Institute of Bioethics and School of Nursing, and Professor of Nursing and Pediatrics, Johns Hopkins University**

"*Change Your Questions* resonates with me because it is not just about knowing the answers but knowing how to ask questions that can transform your life. Dr. Adams's methodology is foundational to everything I do with Appreciative Inquiry and SOAR—it aligns perfectly! Her Choice Map is a valuable resource for anyone who wants to learn the art of inquiry...The book contributes much to the fields of leadership and management...an easy and fun read with real-life examples and insightful wisdom to positively impact your life and the lives of those you lead."

—**Jacqueline M. Stavros, PhD, Professor, Lawrence Technological University; creator of SOAR; and co-editor of *The Appreciative Inquiry Handbook* with David L. Cooperrider and Diana Whitney**

"This book is an invitation to success for individuals and organizations...a surprisingly simple practice to move *away* from judgments that prevent success and *toward* learning that propels us to our goals...practical guidelines for learning organizations."

—**Victoria J. Marsick, PhD, coauthor of** *Sculpting the Learning Organization* **with Karen E. Watkins and Professor of Adult Education, Teachers College, Columbia University**

"*Change Your Questions* is the rare book that I use almost every day. I recently asked Learner questions to quickly transform a delicate organizational situation that for a whole year had seemed intractable... The book changes paradigms, organizations, and lives. It's a classic!"

—**John McAuley, PhD, President and CEO, The Leadership Studio at Muskoka Woods**

"Marilee's work has been a key resource to the World Café since its inception. Essential reading for those committed to their own success in conversations that matter."

—**Juanita Brown, cofounder of The World Café and coauthor of** *The World Café* **with David Isaacs**

"The response to *Change Your Questions* has been overwhelmingly positive. We've shared it across our leadership teams, and we're seeing how it's shifting conversations and having a powerful impact for ourselves and our leaders."

—**Marnie Escaf, Senior Vice President, University Health Network, and Executive Lead, Princess Margaret Cancer Centre, and Petrina McGrath, Vice President, People, Practice and Quality, Saskatoon Health Region**

"If you want to master the art of coaching, you have to master asking great questions. The fastest way to crack open any situation is to use the surgical precision of a smart question. There is no question that Marilee Adams's *Change Your Questions* is your go-to resource!"

—**David Goldsmith, President, Conversant**

"Dr. Adams's writings and her Question Thinking work have contributed significantly to our Kent State Leadership Development Program, which received a Leadership 500 Excellence Award among educational institutions. Our colleagues report many 'lightbulb moments' as a result of *Change Your Questions* and Dr. Adams's superb teaching skills. Question Thinking has totally changed the types of conversations our leaders have and has also led to measurable results in terms of their career trajectories."

—**Robert M. Hall, Director, Training and Organizational Development, Kent State University**

"Marilee demonstrates why Question Thinking is absolutely essential to organizational success...and how easily it can be acquired."

—**Beverly Kaye, PhD, coauthor of *Hello Stay Interviews, Goodbye Talent Loss* with Sharon Jordan-Evans**

"With clarity and accessibility, Dr. Adams models a process whereby we can intentionally change our way of internal inquiry. Imagine being in conscious charge of our own thoughts! A wonderful tool for coaches, leaders, and all helping professionals."

—**Pamela Richarde, MA, Master Certified Coach, Past President, International Coach Federation**

"This fable is destined to be a classic. Buy this book and read it tonight. Your life will never be the same!"

—**Stewart Levine, author of *The Book of Agreement* and *Getting to Resolution***

"I really love this book—and it's one of the most practical I've ever read. The greatest thing is that it's not a 'one and done' kind of book. You'll find yourself going back to it again and again. And you'll definitely find yourself sharing it with friends and colleagues. I know I have."

—**Tracy Davidson, Anchor and Consumer Reporter, NBC 10 News Philadelphia**

"This is a must-read for any leader who wants to ask empowering questions—those that inspire, motivate, and produce positive change... The book can truly change your personal and professional life."

—**Tara Rodas, Manager of Employee Development, Strategic Learning Services Division, Joint Mission Support Center, United States Postal Inspection Service and Office Inspector General**

change
your
questions
change
your life

Inquiry Institute Library Series

Other books by Marilee Adams, Ph.D.

The Art of the Question
A Guide to Short-term Question-Centered Therapy

Teaching That Changes Lives:
Twelve Mindset Tools for Igniting the Love of Learning

MARILEE ADAMS, PH.D.

change
your
questions
change
your life

12 POWERFUL TOOLS
FOR LEADERSHIP,
COACHING, AND LIFE

THIRD EDITION

BK

Berrett–Koehler Publishers, Inc.
San Francisco
a BK Life book

Berrett-Koehler Publishers, Inc.

1333 Broadway, Suite 1000

Oakland, CA 94612-1921

Tel: (510) 817-2277   Fax: (510) 817-2278   www.bkconnection.com

Ordering Information

Quantity sales. Special discounts are available on quantity purchases by corporations,
associations, and others. For details, contact the "Special Sales Department" at the
Berrett-Koehler address above.

Individual sales. Berrett-Koehler publications are available through most bookstores.
They can also be ordered directly from Berrett-Koehler: Tel: (800) 929-2929; Fax: (802)
864-7626; www.bkconnection.com

Orders for college textbook/course adoption use. Please contact Berrett-Koehler: Tel:
(800) 929-2929; Fax: (802) 864-7626.

Orders by U.S. trade bookstores and wholesalers. Please contact Ingram Publisher
Services, Tel: (800) 509-4887; Fax: (800) 838-1149; E-mail: customer.service@ingram-
publisherservices.com; or visit www.ingrampublisherservices.com/Ordering for details
about electronic ordering.

Berrett-Koehler and the BK logo are registered trademarks of Berrett-Koehler Publishers,
Inc.

Printed in the United States of America

Berrett-Koehler books are printed on long-lasting acid-free paper. When it is available,
we choose paper that has been manufactured by environmentally responsible processes.
These may include using trees grown in sustainable forests, incorporating recycled
paper, minimizing chlorine in bleaching, or recycling the energy produced at the paper
mill.

Library of Congress Cataloging-in-Publication Data
Names: Adams, Marilee G., 1945- author.
Title: Change your questions, change your life : 12 powerful tools for
leadership, coaching, and life / Marilee Adams.
Description: Third edition. | Oakland : Berrett-Koehler Publishers,
[2015] |
Includes bibliographical references.
Identifiers: LCCN 2015035976 | ISBN 9781626566330 (pbk.)
Subjects: LCSH: Change (Psychology) | Self-talk.
Classification: LCC BF637.C4 A33 2015 | DDC 158.1--dc23
LC record available at http://lccn.loc.gov/2015035976

Third Edition

20 19 18 17 16 15   10 9 8 7 6 5 4 3 2 1

Book designer: Lisa Devenish
Cover designer: Mark van Bronkhorst / MvB Design
Proofreader: Dianna Haught
Book producer: Detta Penna

FOR ED ADAMS,
my husband and muse

CONTENTS

Marshall Goldsmith

"How can reading *Change Your Questions, Change Your Life* help you and the people who are important to you have better lives—in business and personally?" This is the key question I urge you to keep in mind as you read this invaluable book. The great ideas presented here, in a system of tools Marilee Adams calls *Question Thinking*, provide a solid new way of thinking that can make a positive difference in all our lives.

There are many ideas in this book that helped me. You're sure to find some that will help you, too. *Change Your Questions, Change Your Life* provides methods, skills, and tools for easily implementing Question Thinking both at home and at work. To begin with, Marilee shows how we can become more effective and efficient by focusing on learning rather than being judgmental. As a Buddhist, I know this approach is key to having a happier, more productive life.

Marilee shows us the power of questions to direct our thinking and therefore our actions and results. This means that we can intentionally affect the future by designing the most powerful questions for getting us there. That's what great coaching is all about. It's also what great leaders do—they provide us with visions of new futures. Marilee offers Question Thinking Tools for both coaches and leaders to optimize and fulfill their missions.

It's no surprise that *Change Your Questions, Change Your Life* has become an international bestseller. It's made so much of a real difference in people's lives that they've shared the book with their teams and their companies and also with their families and friends. One of the stories in the Introduction says it all—a reader wrote Marilee that he used the methods in the book so successfully that his company got a mention in *Inc. Magazine*. That's also why so many coaches use the Question Thinking methods and also give the book to their clients.

In my mission as an executive coach, I help successful leaders get better measurable results. This includes teaching a process called *feed forward*. Leaders learn to ask for ideas to move the future. They refine their ability to listen without judgment and to say "thank you" for suggestions. Marilee would call this "listening with Learner ears," which is invaluable for all coaches, leaders, and managers.

Racecar drivers are taught to "focus on the road—not the wall." As you read this book, focus on the road that represents your highest potential by asking questions that lead to a better future, such as: "What are the greatest positive possibilities I can imagine?"

The third edition delivers even more than the first two did. The revisions and the new tools make the material even more accessible and practical. *Change Your Questions, Change Your Life* has great wisdom for us all. Take it very seriously. Roll up your sleeves and get to work. A Buddhist text advises that just reading about a medicine won't bring healing; one actually has to *take* the medicine. So my advice is that the best way to get the most *out* of this book is to practice everything *in* it!

Life is good!

Marshall Goldsmith

Author of the bestselling
What Got You Here Won't Get You There.

Winner of the Harold Longman Award as the
Best Business Book of 2007.

His latest book is *Triggers: Creating Behavior That
Lasts—Becoming the Person You Want to Be.*

The American Management Association named
Dr. Goldsmith as one of 50 great thinkers
and leaders influencing the field of
management over the past 80 years.

Questions for Change

People typically are not aware of their internal
questions or of the profound power they exert in
shaping and directing their experiences and lives.
By changing those questions, one can set in motion
a different process leading to a different result.

David Rock and Linda J. Page

One summer afternoon, shortly after the first edition of
this book was published, I answered my office phone to
hear a man's booming voice announce, "You don't know
me, but I'm Ben." He laughed, and I laughed along with him,
because I knew exactly what he was referring to. Ben is the
main character in *Change Your Questions, Change Your Life,*
and this caller identified with him so much that he thought
I could also help him and his organization.

You see, Ben is almost legendary for many of my readers. Proud of being the "Answer Man," he believes he must
always be the one with the answers and must always be
right. In the story—a business fable through which readers
experience the practical power of *Question Thinking*—Ben
is floundering in his new leadership position. But that isn't
all. He's also having trouble at home. His relationship with
Grace, his wife of less than a year, is growing increasingly

tense. When we first meet him, Ben is one unhappy guy. As the story continues, we learn how he advances in his professional life and deepens his bond with his wife, as he develops the skills of Question Thinking with the help of his coach and mentor, Joseph S. Edwards.

Since that first telephone call from a "Ben," I've received many similar messages from men and women from a wide variety of backgrounds. One reader, David, wrote that like Ben, he'd been in trouble at work, especially with his team. After reading *Change Your Questions* he changed his own questions and, in the process, changed his leadership style. He was ultimately so successful that the results were included in an article in *Inc. Magazine*. You'll find the refer-ence for that article—and others— in the notes at the end of this book.

The first inkling I had of the impact made by *Change Your Questions* occurred when the senior manager at a large pharmaceutical company called me with an invitation to a discussion group featuring my book. She had sent copies to the 50 members of her globally dispersed team with just one instruction: "Come to the book discussion with one exam-ple of *something you've done differently* as a result of reading this book." On the day of the meeting I was ushered into a conference room with about 30 people seated around a large table. Others joined by speakerphone. I listened in amaze-ment as person after person described the results they'd achieved. One man told us he was leading his team more successfully; a woman said that her relationship with a colleague had improved significantly; and a plant manager in Brazil explained how reading the book helped him to recognize and correct a problem in his plant.

Change Your Questions has struck a chord with so many readers that it has become an international bestseller, providing me opportunities to give workshops and keynote presentations in Canada, Europe, and Asia. Largely through word of mouth, the book has become required reading in leadership development programs, coach training institutes, and at universities. It is used by teams in companies and government agencies, by health care professionals in major hospitals, and by Human Resource and Organizational Development professionals. It's used in mediation, marriage enrichment workshops, and in change initiatives with organizations large and small. Readers report that it complements mindfulness practices and emotional intelligence, as well as Appreciative Inquiry, Action Learning, and positive psychology. People share *Change Your Questions* with their partners and children, and with their friends and colleagues.

Question Thinking (QT), the heart of the book, takes on an age-old issue—our ability to be in charge of our own thinking, moment by moment by moment. QT provides skills for observing and assessing our present thinking—especially the questions we're asking ourselves—and then guides us in designing new questions for getting better results. QT helps us think mindfully rather than reactively, leading to more astute choices for productive outcomes, even under pressure. Building reliable capacities for constructive thought is vital for intentional and sustainable change, in both our professional and personal lives. Without this skill, our goals for change may remain only wistful slogans that never come to fruition.

Question Thinking began with an important moment of discovery in my life. I was a determined young graduate student working away on my Ph.D. dissertation. Not only did I endure a ruthless inner critic, but criticisms from others often left me in tears. One fateful day, expecting high praise from my advisor for some work I felt great about, I instead heard from him: "Marilee, this is just not acceptable." At that moment something new happened. Instead of tearfully wondering what was wrong with me, I took a deep breath, and becoming calm and curious, simply asked him "OK, how do I fix it?" That simple shift took me from feeling powerless to being confident enough to take constructive action. Soon I was rewriting the section he had wanted me to change, and to my surprise my inner critic seemed to be taking a rest.

Of course, I had to wonder, "What had happened?! What was so different this time?" I realized that my familiar old judgmental questions about what was wrong and *not good enough* about me seemed to have evaporated. Rather than getting stuck in that quagmire of self-judgment, I had instead focused on the future with the goal of having my writing really work. I had reminded myself of all the good, hard work I had turned in before and that my advisor was on my side.

Was that change of mine just a fluke? Was there a way to turn this seeming miracle into a reliable method for me and others? From such modest beginnings bloomed this body of work that today I call Question Thinking—which points to how we think with questions and how the form of our questions affects our life experiences as well as the results we get. In their book *Coaching with the Brain in Mind: Foundations for Practice*, coauthors David Rock and Linda J. Page described one of the core benefits of my work: "Even what we see as a possibility or action is influenced by our mindset or state of mind. Thus, becoming conscious of and changing our self-questioning is a powerful way to take control of changing our behavior."

Question Thinking provides tools that can help us take charge of our thinking, our emotions, and our behavior not only in our jobs and professions but in every area of our lives. If you're a coach, teaching the QT methodology can become an integral part of each session, providing clients with tools for self-coaching and greater self-awareness. This seamless process is made possible because the tools and methods are highly intuitive and practical.

In the story you'll be reading in the pages ahead, Joseph coaches Ben, who is bumping up against limitations in his leadership skills. Even as Ben moves beyond his limitations, guided by QT principles and tools, Joseph is teaching him how to do this on his own. Thus Ben learns to *self-coach*, a skill that continues to weave its way throughout his life even as he reaps its many benefits.

Change Your Questions is a self-coaching guide for you as much it is for Ben. I've written this book with an emphasis on self-coaching so you can integrate the lessons of QT as you follow Ben's story. Because the book has proven to be so effective for teaching self-coaching, many people in the coaching professions encourage their clients to read it.

But what are the results of this work in the real world, including in organizational life? The most eloquent evidence I can provide are stories shared by my clients and readers. One such story was reported in the *Wharton@Work Newsletter*, which I reference in the Notes at the back of the book. Flextronics is a global leader in electronics manufacturing and distribution in about 30 countries. With goals of culture and behavioral change, Carmella Granado, Senior Director of Organizational Effectiveness, coached the leaders of a poorly performing operations site of about 700 people in the principles of Question Thinking. Before this, the site had had the lowest scores of the 14 others in their division. Carmella assigned the team leaders to read *Change Your Questions* and share the book with their teams. She also coached them with Question Thinking tools to help them brainstorm solutions to current problems.

Within three months, the QT-based coaching that

Carmella provided was credited with the site's dramatic turnaround. They moved to the #1 spot in their division and have maintained a position among the top sites year after year.

People often talk about taking Question Thinking skills home to their families after learning these skills for work. Jason, a workshop participant, told about coming home to find his wife Pam in a panic in his basement office. Water poured down from above, threatening his computer and media equipment. Jason told us, "The old me would have snapped into blame mode." Instead, his Question Thinking skills kicked in. He took a deep breath and told himself, "this is not about blame . . . just figure out what we need to do right now." He quickly shut off the water and called the plumber. Downstairs, a soggy Pam sobbed, "This was your whole world, Jason. And I nearly ruined it." Thanks to learning Question Thinking, Jason said he had the presence of mind to reply, "No, Baby, *you're* my whole world." He later told me, "At that moment I knew it was time to let go of what I'd collected and never let anything get in the way of what was *really* important in my life."

Stories like Ben's, Carmella's, and Jason's help to confirm QT's effectiveness for making significant changes in our personal lives and for growing in our professional lives in positive and sustainable ways. What could be more gratifying for an author than to discover that her work really does make a difference in other people's lives!

When my publisher asked me to write a third edition

of this book, I saw it as a wonderful opportunity to include what I'd learned from my clients, students, and workshop participants. Their contributions have been invaluable on so many different levels, sometimes helping me to see applications of QT I hadn't seen before and often enriching me personally as well.

In many cases I've woven what they've taught me into the book in the form of stories and anecdotes, or used this new knowledge to clarify or enhance the QT tools. Also, in the workbook following the story, you'll find two new tools—one that applies to leadership development and the other to coaching.

In my first book, *The Art of the Question*, I wrote that "with our questions we make the world." Questions open our minds, our eyes, and our hearts. With our questions we learn, connect, and create. We are smarter, more productive, and able to get better results. We shift our orientation from fixed opinions and easy answers to curiosity, thoughtful questions, and open-minded conversations, lighting the way to collaboration, exploration, discovery, and innovation. I have a vision of workplaces and a society—of individuals, families, organizations, and communities—that are vibrant with the spirit of inquiry and possibility.

Now it's time to meet Ben and discover, along with him, how changing your questions really can change your life.

CHAPTER 1

Moment of Truth

If we would have new knowledge, we must get us
a whole new world of new questions.

Susanne K. Langer

A rosewood paperweight on my desk bears a sterling silver plaque declaring: *Great results begin with great questions.* It was a gift from a very special person in my life—Joseph S. Edwards—who introduced me to *Question Thinking,* or *QT,* as he called the skills he taught me. QT opened up a part of my mind that otherwise I might never have discovered. Like everyone else, I believed the way to fix a problem was to look for the right answers. Instead, Joseph showed me that the best way to solve a problem is to *first* come up with better *questions.* The skills he taught me rescued my career and saved my marriage as well. Both were definitely in trouble at the time.

It all started when I was invited to take a position at QTec. The company was in the midst of a major overhaul at the time, and the word on the street was that, barring a miracle, they would fold before the year was out. A friend warned me that accepting a position with QTec would be like signing up to crew on a sinking ship. What convinced me to take the risk? It was my trust in Alexa Harte, the recently appointed CEO at QTec, who'd offered me the position. I'd worked with her for years at KB Corp., my previous employer, where she'd won my respect as a gifted leader. Her confidence about turning QTec around was infectious. Besides, she promised me a great promotion: hefty pay raise, impressive title, and a chance to lead a team in developing an innovative new product. If everything went well the risk would pay off in aces. If not . . . well, I tried not to think about that.

At first I was riding high, convinced I had the job wired. Alexa had hired me for my technology and engineering smarts, and I knew I could deliver on that count. The new product really intrigued me, and the technical challenges were right up my alley. At KB—where Alexa said she'd seen me work miracles—I'd won accolades as the Answer Man. I'd faced down the toughest technical problems, one right after the other. However, at QTec I was also facing a different kind of challenge—heading up a high-stakes, high-visibility team. I was excited about taking this on, although Alexa had let me know I'd have to put effort into developing my people and leadership skills.

My team seemed an enthusiastic and talented bunch, and for a while everything went well. Then life at QTec started unraveling. It was as if suddenly a glaring spotlight was focused on my shortcomings. I didn't dare say it, but secretly I concluded I'd been stuck with a bunch of losers.

To make matters worse, there was Charles. Before I came aboard at QTec he'd been passed over for the job I'd been offered. I could understand why he might resent me. And, just as I expected, he was a real troublemaker from the word go, questioning everything I said and did.

Things went from bad to worse. If the QTec ship wasn't actually sinking, as my friend had warned me was happening, it was definitely taking on water, and I had no idea how to plug up the leaks. My team meetings became a farce—no discussions, no solutions, and no sense of teamwork. And nobody had to remind me that if we couldn't get our product to market before the competition, we would prove the naysayers right.

Life wasn't much better at home. Tension was growing with Grace, my wonderful wife of less than eight months. She constantly asked me about what was going on at work. Finally, one day I just told her she was asking too many questions and she should keep her nose out of my business. She was hurt, I was miserable, and I hadn't the vaguest idea what to do about it.

I didn't want Grace to know how much difficulty I was having. I'd always taken great pride in solving problems that baffled everyone else. This time, with any luck, the right answers would turn up before Grace, Alexa, and the people on my team found out that the job was way over my head.

Meanwhile I kept more and more to myself and did my best to just get through each day.

I was mystified and overwhelmed. It seemed like everything in my life was falling apart. Then came the awful turning point. Grace and I had an argument in the morning, and only hours later there was a major crisis at work. Nobody said it, but I could see it in their eyes: we were cooked.

This was my moment of truth. I needed to be alone and face facts. I called Grace and left a message that I'd be putting in an all-nighter to finish an important report. Then I spent the whole long night in my office, staring at the walls, still searching desperately for the right answers and reliving the most disastrous weeks of my life. I told myself I had to face the truth: I had failed. Just after six that morning I went out for coffee and then started drafting my resignation. I finished three hours later, called Alexa, and made arrangements to see her immediately.

The walk to Alexa's suite was less than a hundred yards. That morning it felt like a hundred miles. When I got to the big double doors of her office I stopped and took a deep breath to regain my composure. I stood there for some long moments, working up the nerve to knock. Just as I was raising my arm, I heard a voice behind me.

"Ben Knight, you're here. Good, good!"

It was Alexa. There was no mistaking that voice, always cheerful, exuding a sense of optimism even when things were going badly. An attractive, athletic-looking woman in her late 40s, she radiated confidence. I'd told Grace that

I'd never met anyone quite like Alexa. She approached her responsibilities at QTec with boundless enthusiasm. It wasn't that she didn't take her job seriously. She took it very seriously! And she did it with such pleasure and self-assurance that she made it look easy.

At that moment, her mere presence made me acutely aware of my deficiencies. I felt numb, barely mumbling a subdued good morning as she touched my shoulder and ushered me into her office.

The room was expansive, the size of a large living room in the best executive home. I crossed deep green carpeting, soft underfoot, and walked over to the large bay window where the meeting area was set up. There, two overstuffed sofas faced each other across a large walnut coffee table.

"Sit!" Alexa said, gesturing in a welcoming way to one of the couches." Betty said your lights were on when she left her office at seven-thirty last night, and you were here when she came in early this morning."

She sat down across from me on the other couch.

"I presume that's for me?" Alexa asked, pointing to the green folder containing my resignation that I'd placed on the coffee table.

I nodded, waiting for her to pick it up. Instead, she leaned back, looking as if she had all the time in the world.

"Tell me what's going on with you," she said.

I pointed to the green folder. " It's my resignation. I'm sorry, Alexa."

The next sound I heard stopped me cold. It was not a gasp, not a word of reproach, but laughter! It was not cruel laughter, either. What had I missed? I didn't understand. How could Alexa still sound sympathetic in the face of all I'd screwed up?

"Ben," she said, "you're not going to quit on me." She slid the folder in my direction. "Take this back. I know more about your situation than you realize. I want you to give me at least a few months. But for that period of time, you've got to commit to making changes."

"Are you sure about this?" I asked, dumbfounded.

"Let me answer you this way," she continued. "Many years ago, I was in a situation similar to yours. I had to face facts. If I wanted to be successful I'd need to make some fundamental changes. I was pretty desperate. A man by the name of Joseph sat me down and asked some straightforward questions, simple ones on the surface. But those questions opened doors I never even knew existed. He asked, 'Are you willing to take responsibility for your mistakes—and for the attitudes and actions that led to them?' Then he said, 'Are you willing—however begrudgingly—to forgive yourself, and even laugh at yourself?' And finally, 'Will you look for value in your experiences, especially the most difficult ones?' Bottom line: 'Are you willing to learn from what happened and make changes accordingly?' "

She went on to tell me how Joseph's work with her, and the methods he had developed over the years, had changed not only her life but her husband Stan's as well." Stan has more than tripled his net worth in the past few years. He attributes the success he and his company enjoy today to what Joseph taught him. Joseph will probably tell you all about it. He loves to tell stories, especially ones about how people's lives were changed by changing their questions."

I must have looked perplexed because she added, "Don't worry about what I mean by *questions that change people's lives*. You'll learn about that soon enough." She paused. Then, in carefully measured words, she said, "I want you to work with my friend Joseph, starting immediately. I'm sure he'll want to meet with you over a period of time. Figure out the schedule with him. This is top priority now."

"What is he, a therapist?" The idea of seeing a shrink made me nervous.

Alexa smiled. "No, he's an executive coach. I call him an *inquiring coach*."

Inquiring coach! If I knew anything at all, it was that I needed answers, not more questions. How could more questions possibly benefit me or pull me out the hole I was in?

As I was getting ready to leave, Alexa jotted something down on a piece of paper and sealed it in an envelope. "Inside this envelope is a prediction I've made," she said mysteriously, handing it to me. "Put it in that green folder of yours and don't open it until you've completed your work with Joseph and I tell you it's the time to open it." Then she gave me Joseph's business card. I turned it over. There was a big question mark on the other side. It really irritated me. The idea that I'd be spending valuable time with a man whose logo was a question mark went against everything I believed.

Back in my own office, I collapsed in the chair behind my desk. My eyes fell on a small gilded frame on the wall. It held a saying, just two words long: *Question everything!* It was a quote attributed to Albert Einstein. Many rooms at QTec contained a framed placard exactly like this one. As much as I respected and appreciated Alexa's leadership, this message had always been a point of contention for me. Everybody knows that leaders should have *answers*, not questions.

My eyes were fixed on Joseph's card with the question mark on the back. What had I gotten myself into? Only time would tell. At least I could put off my decision to resign. My attention shifted to Grace. How was I ever going to smooth things over with her? At that moment there was only one thing to be grateful for—Alexa hadn't asked about Grace and me. I think that would have been the last straw. I knew Alexa was fond of my wife—she'd even come to our wedding. She wouldn't have been happy to find out we were having trouble.

I sat there for a long time just staring at Joseph's card. The fact that Alexa had refused to accept my resignation offered a little hope. I was encouraged that she would refer me to her own mentor—even though the jury was still out on whether her trust in me was justified. Still, I had nothing to lose by keeping an appointment with this inquiring coach guy. Besides, even though I was skeptical, I was also curious. If this Joseph guy had helped Alexa and Stan so much, maybe he had answers that would help me, too.

"Question everything!"

Albert Einstein

CHAPTER 2

A Challenge Accepted

What got you here won't get you there.

Marshall Goldsmith

My appointment with Joseph S. Edwards was at ten the next morning. I didn't tell Grace about this meeting or about my conversation with Alexa. And I certainly didn't tell her about writing my resignation. Admitting I was in trouble had never come easily. I preferred working things out on my own. For some time now I'd been stonewalling Grace and feeling more and more resentful about her constant questions about what was going on with me. Until I found the right answers and solutions I was determined to tough it out and keep my problems to myself. But as usually happened with Grace, I wasn't so good at hiding my problems.

I should have realized that she knew something more than the usual job stress was bothering me. That morning, on our way to the airport, where Grace was catching a plane for a lunch meeting in another city, she brought things to a head. As I pulled up to the curb at the terminal, she told me,

"I've been feeling like a widow lately. You've been so distant and moody. Ben, if you want a real partnership with me, you're going to have to make some changes."

God knows I love Grace but I wasn't in the best of moods.

"I don't need this right now," I told her, more harshly than I intended.

Grace looked stunned. I got out of the car to get her brief-case from the trunk. As I handed it to her our eyes met, and for a moment I was afraid she was going to cry. I knew it wasn't right leaving her like that, but I was feeling pushed. Besides, if I got dragged into a long discussion, I'd be late for my appoint-ment with Joseph. Our little problem would have to wait. Grace forced a smile, told me she'd be back that night but not to worry about picking her up. She'd get a taxi home. She turned and quickly disappeared into the crowd.

I was angry. *Why did she have to choose this particular morning to pick a fight?* I hit the accelerator and pulled out into traffic. Horns blasted. I slammed on my brakes as some maniac raced by, barely missing me. I was fuming. Between that near collision, the conflict with Grace, and having to attend a meet-ing I dreaded, my morning was off to a very bad start.

Joseph's office was in the Pearl Building downtown, a 14-story edifice constructed in the 1930s and recently restored. Old Town, as we called the area, was a bustling shopping center with great places to eat and drink, and unusual little stores. Grace and I often had dinner there, at a small place called the Metropol. Grace is an art lover, and she'd opened up a whole new world I'd hardly known existed. Thanks to her, we'd spent many happy hours together, browsing through bookstores and art galleries. Passing our familiar haunts that morning, I worried about what the future held for us.

I pushed open the polished brass-framed doors at the Pearl Building, crossed the marble floors, and caught an elevator to Joseph's penthouse office. I stepped into a large foyer that looked like someone's private residence. Several tall ficus trees reached up toward a large skylight.

Beyond this private anteroom, a double set of doors opened invitingly to a long hallway. On the walls hung some kind of artwork. I remember thinking that Grace would enjoy seeing this.

"You must be Ben Knight!" Joseph Edwards strode toward me enthusiastically. I judged him to be in his early 60s, though he moved like an agile sprinter a quarter that age. No more than 5 feet 9, he was dressed casually, wearing an outrageous knit sweater with a myriad of striped patterns that dazzled the eye. He was not at all like I'd expected.

Joseph's smooth-shaven face glowed with good humor. His brown eyes sparkled with almost childlike excitement. Atop his head, a wild array of woolly white curls reminded me of photos I'd seen of Albert Einstein in his later years.

Joseph's warm welcome dissolved some of my reservations about spending time with him. He led me down the hallway to his office, explaining as we went that the walls displayed "some artifacts I call my *Question Thinking Hall of Fame.*" What I had at first mistaken for pictures were actually framed magazine articles and letters. I didn't get a good look at them. We turned left into a large room bathed in the morning sunlight.

The room contained comfortable seating, a well-used brick fireplace, and a walnut conference table with matching chairs. One wall displayed certificates and a few dozen autographed photos, many with their subjects shaking hands with Joseph. In the pictures I recognized faces I'd seen in the news over the years. Alexa hadn't quite prepared me for this. Joseph was obviously very well connected in the business world and beyond.

I also saw covers of three different books displayed in elegant frames. They were all written by Joseph. Each had the words *Question Thinking* in the title. One in particular caught my eye. It was coauthored with a Sarah Edwards and was about *inquiring marriages.*

I was impressed but also intimidated. We entered a less formal room, where I felt slightly more comfortable. Windows on three sides afforded a spectacular view of the city. In the distance, wispy clouds were lifting from the woods. The views seemed to stretch on forever.

I eased myself into a large leather armchair while Joseph took his place near me in a matching one. He dangled a pair of rimless reading glasses from his left hand.

After some brief get-acquainted conversation, he asked, "Tell me, what do you suppose is your greatest asset?"

"I'm the Answer Man, the Go-To guy," I told him with pride. "I've built my whole career around being the person people go to for answers. The bottom line for me is answers and results. That's what business is all about."

"True. But how can you get the best answers without asking the best questions first?" Joseph paused, placing his glasses on his nose and peering over the top of them at me: "Is there a single question you would say characterizes the way you operate?"

How can you get the best answers without asking the best questions first?

"Sure," I said. "Get the right answers and be ready to back them up, that's my motto."

Joseph asked me to restate that as a question, one I would ask myself. I couldn't see the point, but I did as he asked, "Okay. Sure. The question I operate with is, *How can I prove I'm right?*

"That's great," Joseph said. "Then we might have your problem nailed already."

"My problem?"

"Being the answer man. Having to prove you're right," Joseph said. "I must say, Ben, we're getting down to business faster than I expected."

I wasn't sure if I'd heard him correctly. *Was he kidding?* No, he was dead serious. "I beg your pardon?"

"Finding proof that our answers are correct can be important," he said. "But would you allow that there are times when too much of a good thing can get you in trouble? For example, how do you think your having to be right all the time goes over with your team?"

"I'm not sure what you mean," I said, and I really meant it. I wanted my team to find answers, the correct answers. "Everyone's looking for answers." That's what we all get paid to do, isn't it?

"Let me get personal for a moment," Joseph said. "Do your efforts to prove you're right work with your wife?"

That one hit home. "Not really," I admitted. Grace had told me how my habit of insisting on being right often frustrated her.

"It doesn't work so well with my wife either," Joseph said smiling. "With that in mind, let's look a little deeper into what questions really do. Certainly we recognize that questions are a vital part of communication. But the role they play in thinking is not always obvious, and that's where Question Thinking skills can be invaluable.

"If you're willing to grab onto the real power of questions, they can change your whole life. It comes down to increasing the quantity and quality of the questions we ask ourselves and one another. It also matters enormously what our intentions are when we ask those questions. As the Romanian playwright Eugène Ionesco famously said, '*It is not the answer that enlightens, but the question.*'"

I must have looked puzzled, because Joseph paused and said, "You've never heard the term *Question Thinking* before, have you?"

I shook my head, no.

"Question Thinking is a system of skills and tools using questions to expand how you approach virtually any situation. You develop the skills to refine your questions for vastly better results in anything you do. That begins with asking questions of ourselves and only then asking them of others. The QT system, that is, Question Thinking, can literally put action into your thinking—action that's focused, creative, and effective. It's a great way to create a foundation for making wiser choices."

"Go on," I said, skeptically.

"Much of the time we're barely conscious of asking questions, especially the ones we ask ourselves. But questions are a part of our thought process nearly every moment of our lives. Thinking actually occurs as an internal question-and-answer process. Not only that, we often answer our own questions by taking some action, by doing something.

"Here's an example. When you got dressed this morning, I'll bet you went to your closet, or dresser—or maybe even the floor—and asked yourself questions like: *Where am I going? What's the weather? What's comfortable?* Or even, *What's clean?* You answered your questions by making a quick decision and then *doing* something. You selected some clothing and put it on. You are, in effect, wearing your answers."

"I guess I can't argue with that. As you say, though, if I did ask those questions, I hardly noticed it at the time. Actually, my biggest question was whether Grace picked up my clothes at the cleaners, like she promised."

We both laughed.

Question Thinking is a system of tools for transforming thinking, action, and results through skillful question asking— questions we ask ourselves as well as those we ask others.

Joseph was on a roll. It seemed like a good idea to just sit back and hear him out. Besides, I was actually getting interested.

"When we get stuck," Joseph continued, "it's natural to go on a hunt for answers and solutions. But in doing so we often unintentionally put up blocks instead of creating openings. I always remember that wonderful quote of

Albert Einstein's: 'We cannot solve our problems with the same thinking we used when we created them.' To solve our problems, we first need to change our questions; otherwise we'll probably just keep getting the same old answers, over and over again.

"We cannot solve our problems with the same thinking we used when we created them."

Albert Einstein

"New questions can totally shift our perspectives, moving us into fresh ways of looking at problems. Questions have even changed the course of events. Let me give you a dramatic example. Think about this. Long ago, nomadic societies were driven by the implicit question *How do we get ourselves to water?*"

I nodded. "Which is what kept them nomadic . . ."

"Yet look what happened when their implicit question changed to *How do we get water to come to us?* That new question initiated one of humanity's most significant paradigm shifts. It ushered in agriculture, including the invention of irrigation, the storage of water, digging wells, and eventually the creation of cities, often many miles from water. Just think of Las Vegas. That new question changed peoples' behavior, changed the course of history, and we can never go back."

"I guess I can see how questions apply to getting dressed and even to that paradigm shift for nomads. But how does this apply to business? And more to the point, how can it help *me* with my problems?"

"The point is that questions drive results," Joseph responded. "They virtually program how we think and behave and what kinds of outcomes are possible. Consider three companies, each one driven by one of the following questions: *What's the best way to satisfy shareholders? What's the best way to satisfy customers? What's the best way to satisfy employees?* In terms of a business, each question takes our mind in a different direction. Each question will have a different influence on priorities, everyday behavior, and strategies for achieving goals. Remember: *Questions drive results.* That's as true in your day-to-day life at QTec as it was for nomads thousands of years ago.

Questions drive results.

"Your ideas are interesting," I hedged. "But I've literally built my reputation on having answers . . . not questions."

"Fortunately," Joseph continued, "the route from being an answer man to becoming a question man is much shorter than you might think."

What was he suggesting? Giving up my cherished role as the answer man was about the furthest thing from my mind. I wasn't about to give up something that had worked so well for me for so long. One thing I was pretty certain of—if we'd stuck with only questions, we'd still be scratching our heads and hunting for our suppers with pointed sticks.

Joseph removed his glasses and paused, as if contemplating what he was going to say next. Then he spoke in a slow, even voice.

"Ben, you've got to face facts here—you're in trouble. One of your greatest assets—being the answer man—has turned into a liability. That's the bottom line."

As Joseph spoke, I imagined Grace sitting here in his office with me. Truly, she would applaud what he was saying. A big knot tightened in my belly.

"If being the answer man was still working for you," Joseph continued, "you wouldn't have spent the night in your office writing your resignation. Alexa told me about that. I know where you were coming from. I've had my own share of all-night debates with the walls of my office.

"This is where I think I can help you," he said. "Alexa has been watching your career for a long time. She believes you've got great potential, and she's obviously invested a lot in you. But she also thinks that without some big changes you won't make it as a leader at QTec. She knows you pretty well, Ben. Before she hired you she shared her concerns with me about bringing you into the company. She especially had questions about your readiness for a leadership position. If I'm not mistaken, she also told you what she was worried about. Alexa is not exactly a shrinking violet."

We both laughed at that comment, and I was grateful for a moment of levity. Alexa was about the most forthright human being I'd ever met. She never beat around the bush.

With more than a little embarrassment, I remembered her exact words the day she hired me: "Ben, I'm bringing you in because you're absolutely the best in your field. I'm completely confident about your technical acumen, which we need for the new markets we plan to open up. What I'm not as comfortable with is your people skills. That's where you need to improve if you're going to make it as a leader. I'm gambling on you and I'm planning on winning this bet."

At the time, I had brushed off Alexa's warning. Instead, I had immediately called Grace to tell her about my great *coup*. If I'd heard Alexa's warning at all, it was filtered through the plans I was making for a victory celebration with my wife that evening.

"As an answer man," Joseph said, "your dogged determination to find the right answers has led you to some brilliant breakthroughs. However, the line between having the right answers and being perceived as a know-it-all can indeed be thin. You could even come off as arrogant and uncaring. My guess is that with the added pressure and responsibility of your new position, that know-it-all style has gotten exaggerated. Once you get labeled, you're in trouble. When others start seeing you that way, can you really expect them to like or respect you? It's not exactly an ideal leadership profile."

"Who's running a popularity contest here?" I countered. In my mind, a good leader has one responsibility— get the job done and see that others follow through on their assignments. Nobody on my team was producing.

"Whenever you're interacting with other people as a leader," Joseph said, "you want them to take initiative, ask questions, and come up with answers that maybe you hadn't thought of yourself. Your accomplishments come from the total efforts of the people you're working with, not just from your own solitary work. The skills that allowed you to create such dazzling technological breakthroughs in the past are not the same skills you need to be successful as a leader. In the words of Marshall Goldsmith, 'What got you here won't get you there.'"

Joseph went to his desk and took something from the side drawer. As he handed it to me I read the title: *Question Thinking Workbook*. I began flipping through the pages.

"If it's true that you're coming across as a know-it-all," he continued, "which is the downfall of the Answer Man, you don't leave much room for anyone else. You're great at the technical stuff, Ben, but your present job requires much more than that. You're working with people, not objects. Where people are concerned, there's a certain magic in getting just the right mixture between questions and answers.

I can offer this suggestion: Start by *asking* more and *telling* a lot less. The most effective communication is much more about asking and much less about telling. Unless you do ask questions, how can you make room for new information or find out what people are thinking or needing? Conventional wisdom has it upside down—in fact, even most formal communication courses usually focus on telling and not nearly enough on the importance of asking questions.

"For you, Ben, it's vital to get curious and ask more questions—not just about technical matters but especially about people. Start asking yourself questions like: *What can I do to get people more engaged? What can I do to get people working collaboratively? What do others need from me? What do they have to contribute that I haven't been noticing?*"

"Seems to me you're putting way too much emphasis on questions," I said. "Everyone has questions. That's a no-brainer. But in my experience it's the guy with answers who makes things happen."

"Face it, Ben, you've hit a wall. Are you going to climb over it? Alexa is convinced you will. It's your choice, not mine, so I can't answer that question for you. Here are some more questions you might ask yourself: *Do I really listen to people's questions and suggestions? Do people feel like I listen to their questions and suggestions? Do they feel respected by me? Do they feel invited to take risks and share their ideas?*"

Joseph paused. "You look perplexed," he said. "Want to share what's going on with you?"

It took me a moment to collect my thoughts. The truth is, I hadn't expected this meeting to get so personal. When I asked myself those questions about my interactions with other people, I was taken aback, though I still didn't get the point. "All this theory might be fine," I finally managed to say, "but these soft skills just seem, well, *soft*. I thought we'd be discussing something really practical, something to get actual results, to turn things around."

Joseph laughed in a friendly way. "Don't underestimate the power of soft skills. As a mutual friend of ours once said, 'We ignore soft skills at our peril. Developing these skills can be the difference that makes the difference between success and failure.'"

"That sounds like Alexa," I said.

Joseph nodded. "In today's world it's not enough to have top technical expertise, or to have the best training in any of the so-called hard skills. Leaders need interpersonal and relationship-building skills, skills for communicating more effectively and constructively. Think of these so-called soft skills, or people skills, as the keystone of leadership success. The good news is that these are learnable skills."

We ignore soft skills at our peril. Developing these skills can be the difference that makes the difference between success and failure.

"You and I have very different ways of thinking," I said. "You think in questions. I think in answers. You're going to have to prove to me that this Question Thinking stuff can be practical enough to make a difference with my problems."

"Fair enough," Joseph said. "Let's start with another question: Would you agree that you're looking for ways to change?"

I shrugged. "Isn't the fact that I'm here proof enough that I'm looking for changes?" Truthfully, I was thinking *what kind of nonsense is he promoting here?* But I didn't say it. I didn't say anything.

"To change something, you need to first understand where you're starting from. The better you can observe that, the more effective you'll be with making the changes you want. And that's where Question Thinking can help you. Really effective, intentional change begins with strengthening your *observer self.* The better you can see what's going on—that's where the observer self comes in—the better you can apply the right skills and strategies to make the changes you want."

Joseph's emphasis on the observer self piqued my interest. I was familiar with using this observer part of myself to solve technical problems by looking at what was working, what wasn't working, and coming up with answers to solve a problem. But I had never looked through that observer lens when it came to how I interact with other people. I'd hardly given much thought to developing people skills much less that they were actually skills you could learn.

"There's a tool in the workbook for honing your skills as an observer," Joseph said. "That's the first tool. Before we meet next time, read it over and think about it."

I nodded absently as I searched for the place he was talking about in the workbook. Ready or not, the self-observing questions were already coming. First and foremost was, "Should I be questioning my assumption about the power of answers?" I was beginning to suspect I might miss something important if I didn't listen carefully to Joseph. The notion that Grace might agree with him was also playing at the back of my mind. Was I doing too much *telling* and not enough *asking* with her? I suspect I already knew the answer to that question.

"Judging by the look on your face, I'm guessing you're a little unsettled right now," Joseph said. "But I assure you that once you understand how to use the Question Thinking principles and practices, particularly in strengthening your ability to observe yourself, all the pieces will fall into place. Think of this workbook as a guide into this world of questions. I promise that these tools provide a practical *how-to* that makes real change possible. You have no idea what a powerful difference this can make for your career." Joseph flashed me an enigmatic smile and added, "To say nothing of what it can do for your personal relationships."

Question Thinking! This was going to be a challenge. Even Joseph's terms for his theories got to me. Wasn't it bad enough that he wanted me to ask myself and other people more questions? I admit my reaction was a bit juvenile, but I felt like covering my ears with my hands. Almost immediately a question popped into my head: *Was my resistance getting in the way of listening openly to what he had to offer?* No matter. It was time to bite the bullet. I had to try what he had to offer. What choice did I have? I was desperate.

"Let's be clear about this," Joseph said. "This system of tools and practices is *not* psychotherapy, but you can think of it as learning how to coach yourself through challenges to get better results. It's about becoming more efficient, productive, creative, and successful, and it's about leading others toward those ends," Joseph continued, "and I think you'll agree there's nothing more practical than that. In the end, I believe you'll be able to make a quantum leap out of your present quandary. Despite any doubts you might have at the present time, I'm with Alexa on this one. I'm betting on your success."

At this point Joseph declared a half-hour intermission, as he jokingly called it. I made a quick call back to my office. There was nothing that couldn't wait, which was a relief. I was feeling pretty shaken up.

I decided that when I left Joseph's office I would go to a quiet coffee shop, skim his workbook, and think about my next moves. Did Joseph understand the importance of my strengths as an answer man? Was I missing something? Was *he*?

Minutes later, standing in the mirrored elevator, I looked up and caught my reflection. Staring back at me was the face of a stranger filled with tension and frustration—me! Was this the face that Grace had been looking at for the past few months? Truth be told, I wasn't sure I'd want to hang around that guy myself. Could I really change, as Alexa and Joseph seemed to believe? And did I really want to? Maybe I should accept my strengths as a guy who's an expert on answers. Maybe I really wasn't leadership material.

CHAPTER 3

The Choice Map

Maps don't just help us locate where we are
but where we are coming from and where
we might be going.

Gabrielle Roth

When we resumed our conversation, Joseph pointed to a mural on his office wall. I'd noticed it before but hadn't paid much attention to it. "This is the Choice Map," he explained. (It appears later in this chapter.) "It helps us to become better observers of the two basic paths we take in life—the Learner Mindset path and the Judger Mindset path. As the name implies, the map is all about our ability to make choices. On the left side of the Choice Map, notice the figure standing above the Start arrow, at the crossroads between the two paths. That figure represents you and me—every one of us. In every moment of our lives we're faced with choosing between the Learner Mindset path and the Judger Mindset path. Now look at the thought bubble above the other figures' heads. Note how there's a relationship between the kinds of questions these people ask, the path they're on, and where each path takes them."

Joseph then directed my attention to two little signs near that Start arrow on the left of the map: The sign above the Learner Mindset path said "Choose"; the sign by the Judger Mindset path said "React." I looked at the Learner Mindset path with the figures happily jogging along. That path, associated with *choosing*, looked pretty inviting to me.

I then looked at the Judger Mindset path, with the sign that said React. The figures there looked downright troubled and bleak as the path took them toward the billboard labeled *Judger*. No happy joggers here. And then I noticed that fellow sinking in the mud of the *Judger Pit*. I started to chuckle but then swallowed hard. *Was this Joseph's impression of me?* My shoulders tightened up. *What if he was right?*

"I hope you're not thinking I'm like that loser in the Judger Pit," I said guardedly.

"You wouldn't be in this office if anybody believed you were a loser," Joseph replied. "Every single one of us has Judger moments, including me. It's a natural part of being human. The Choice Map is about observing yourself and others in a more conscious way; it's about helping us to see what path we're on at any moment. It's not about labeling people or putting them in boxes. Think of the Choice Map* as a tool that helps us to chart more effective paths through our lives—and for getting better outcomes in whatever we do."

I began to relax a little.

---

*Readers of this book can download a free color copy of the Choice Map at: www.InquiryInstitute.com. Use code: CYQ3.

"At nearly every moment of our lives, we're faced with choosing between taking the Learner or Judger path," Joseph continued. "Whether we recognize it or not, we're making choices moment by moment by moment. Those choices take us along the Learner path or the Judger Path. These are our mindsets. As you can see, by choosing Learner mindset we can discover new possibilities. By jumping into Judger mindset we can eventually end up stuck in the mud.

"Most of the time, we're shifting back and forth between Learner and Judger mindsets, barely aware we have any control or choice. Choice begins when we are mindful enough to observe our own thoughts and feelings and the language we use to express them. This is the key to success— building the muscles of the observer self. Self-coaching is impossible without a strong observer! It's as simple as asking ourselves, *What's going on? Where am I right now? Am I in Judger or Learner?* Choice begins with observing our own thinking, and our own mindsets. It's simpler than you think."

I nodded, still skeptical.

"Let's put it to the test," Joseph said. "We've got a perfect issue to work with, too. Look at what happened in that moment when you asked if I thought you were a loser and a Judger."

"Okay," I said, nodding uneasily.

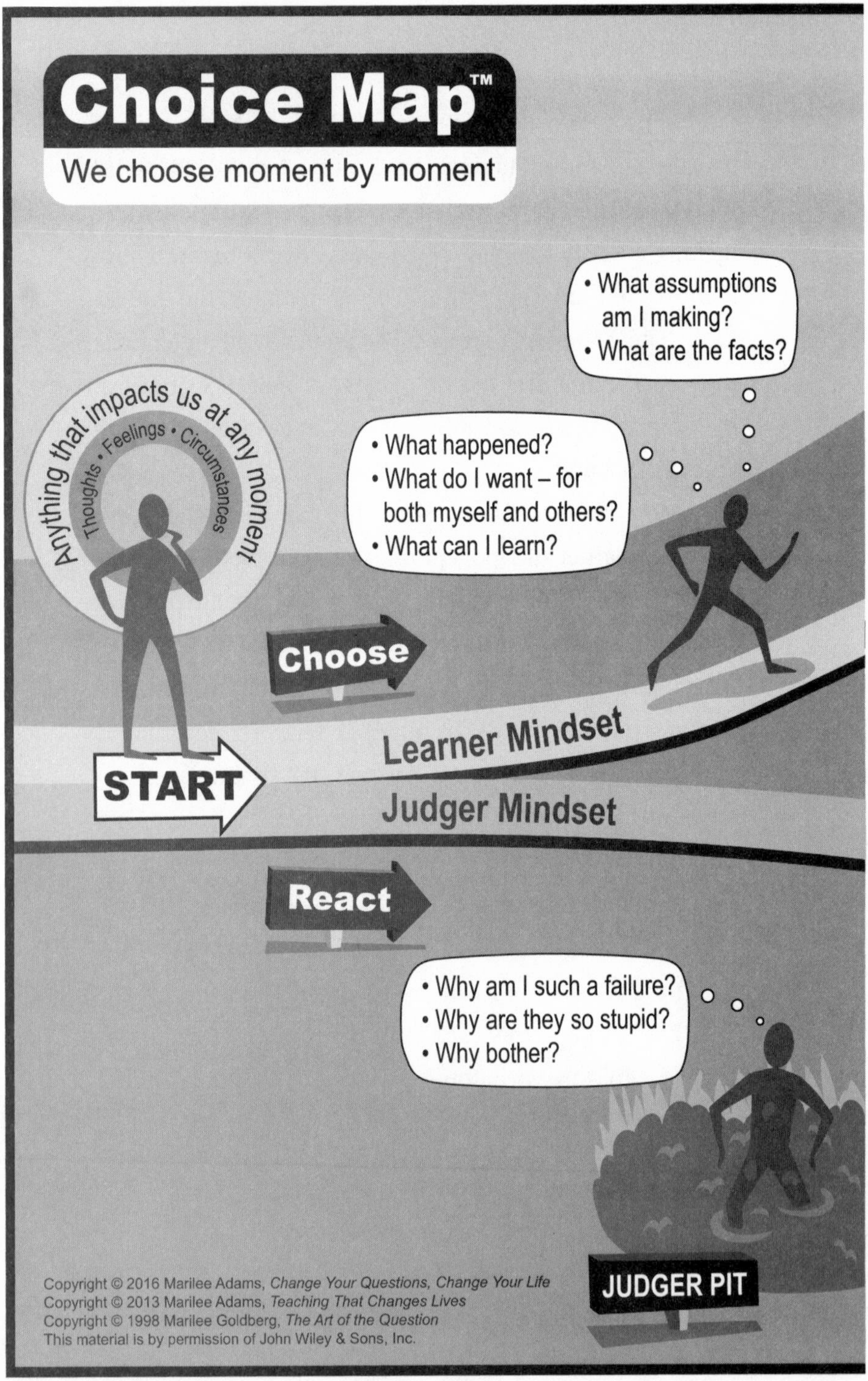

Choice Map™
We choose moment by moment
Anything that impacts us at any moment
Thoughts • Feelings • Circumstances
• What assumptions am I making?
• What are the facts?
• What happened?
• What do I want – for both myself and others?
• What can I learn?
Choose
START
Learner Mindset
Judger Mindset
React
• Why am I such a failure?
• Why are they so stupid?
• Why bother?
JUDGER PIT
Copyright © 2016 Marilee Adams, Change Your Questions, Change Your Life
Copyright © 2013 Marilee Adams, Teaching That Changes Lives
Copyright © 1998 Marilee Goldberg, The Art of the Question
This material is by permission of John Wiley & Sons, Inc.

"Imagine that it's you standing at the crossroads between the Learner and Judger paths," Joseph said, pointing to that Start arrow on the Choice Map. "Notice the words that circle that figure's head—*Anything that impacts us at any moment.* That can be *Thoughts, Feelings, Circumstances.* The circumstances might be something unpleasant, such as getting an unexpected bill or a phone call with distressing news. Maybe a truck scraped the fender of your new car in the parking lot. The whole world begins to look like that mud pit at the end of the Judger path. Stuff happens. Right?"

I rolled my eyes and thought, *he doesn't know the half of it!*

"But circumstances that feel positive impact us, too," Joseph continued. "Your favorite team has an unexpected win. Your boss gives you a promotion, or your spouse sends an invitation to spend a romantic evening together."

"I could stand more of the good stuff!" I grumbled. "So what's the point here?"

"Things happen to us all the time," Joseph said. "We don't have much choice about that but we *do* have choice about what we do next about whatever just happened. Case in point: let's examine what happened the exact moment when I first showed you the Choice Map. Just looking at it led to thoughts and feelings that put you on the Judger Path. What do *you* think happened?"

"I don't know," I said. "Something just pushed my buttons and off I went." I remembered the questions that ran through my mind at that moment: *Does Joseph think I'm a Judger and a loser? Does he think I'm like that guy sinking in the mud?*

"Yeah, I admit it," I said. "I went into a pretty bad mindset."

"Whoa!" Joseph exclaimed. "There's no good or bad, no right or wrong here. There's just observing what happens and what you do with what happens. Remember the little signs at the beginning of the paths—Choose and React. In those first instants, you reacted to what happened and bombarded yourself with negative Judger questions."

"Am I a hopeless case?" I said, cracking a feeble smile.

Joseph smiled back. "That's a good example of a negative Self-Question, or Self-Q, as I call them, which sends us right into the Judger Pit."

"So how do I get out?"

"You observe your mindset and then choose. I believe that the secret of being really effective and satisfied in our lives begins with our ability to distinguish between Judger and Learner. That's a key part of Question Thinking. Change your questions, change your thinking. Change your thinking, change your results. If only for a second, you become an observer watching a movie of your life. You simply notice whatever moods, thoughts, and behaviors are going on, without interpretation or judgment. That mindfulness sets the stage for just accepting what is, which also sets the stage for change, for choosing the mindset you're going to operate from. This is very different from being so immersed in the situation that you can't imagine any other possibility than the way it already is."

I nodded. "With engineering problems, I use something like this observer self to cross-check my calculations and conclusions and make sure I haven't missed anything. You're saying the Choice Map gives me a way of developing this observer self to cross-check *myself*— to observe whatever moods and thoughts might be shaping my choices—not just about numbers but also about myself and other people. That gives me the power to make a course correction."

"Exactly! I'm sure you've had the experience of catching yourself calling somebody by the wrong name or nearly putting your foot in your mouth. We all do it. It's your observer self that catches the error. You see, it's a natural capacity, something everyone has—and the Choice Map increases that capacity. It gives us a chance to focus on the bigger picture. Until you develop this ability you're running on automatic pilot, reacting mindlessly. The Choice Map is about developing ways to make intentional, conscious choices rather than being controlled by events around us or by our emotions. These are essential leadership qualities for being aware, awake, and responsive to the business at hand."

Joseph paused. Then his face broke into a smile. "Let me tell you a little story about me," he said. "A few months ago I was in a coaching session with the superintendent of a large construction company. I spent 15 long minutes listening to his complaining and putting down everyone and blaming all his company's woes on everybody else. According to him, the world is filled with idiots. I was getting pretty fed up with all his judgmental chatter. I felt like kicking him out of my office! Judger questions were coursing wildly through my mind. *What did I do to deserve this guy? Who does he think he is, God's gift to mankind?* When I suddenly realized what I was doing I almost laughed out loud. Here I was judging this man for judging other people! I was in Judger mindset as much as he was. I'd been hijacked by Judger! Going Judger on Judger is a real trap."

Joseph obviously enjoyed telling this story on himself. "So how did the Choice Map help?" I wanted him to tell me the whole process.

"First, you just notice that something's not quite right," he said. "Maybe you feel tense, or upset, or just plain blocked. That's your observer self starting to click in, making you more aware. Then you ask yourself, *Am I in Judger? Is this where I want to be?* Of course, in the story I'm telling you, it wasn't. If I stayed in Judger, I couldn't help this guy. *No one can help anyone else from a Judger place.*"

No one can help anyone else from a Judger place.

"Sounds like you should have cut your losses and backed out," I suggested.

"Not at all," Joseph replied. "As soon as our observer self recognizes we're in Judger, that's when we begin to gain control and personal power. Now we have choice. We can choose to switch our thinking from Judger to Learner. There's a specific kind of question that helps us here; it's what I call a *Switching question*. That's what provides the how-to for changing. The Switching question that worked for me that day was, *How else can I think about him?*

"That question gave me the freedom to wonder: *What does he need?* Instead of wanting to write him off, that question helped me to become curious about him. The Choice Map simplifies this whole process for observing yourself. You discover more options and can choose more wisely, even under pressure. Choosing is easy when things are going well. It's when we're under pressure that we really get tested."

Something in what he said made me think about that awful moment with Grace at the airport. "It seems like people go into Judger whenever there's any kind of conflict," I reflected. "I mean, both people go Judger at the same time. That's pretty normal, isn't it?"

"Very normal," Joseph said. "And then everything escalates and the possibility of a good resolution comes to a screeching halt. But here's a million dollar tip for you: *When two people are in Judger, the one who wakes up first has an advantage.* That person can choose to go Learner and turn the situation around for both of them."

When two people are in Judger, the one who wakes up first has an advantage. That person can choose to go Learner and turn the situation around for both of them.

Something clicked for me. When Grace and I had a disagreement, she would often switch from stubbornness to open-mindedness in the blink of an eye. Her ability to switch always lightened things up. I had often wondered if she did this naturally or if it was some inner trick. She once told me she just took a deep breath and reminded herself of the big picture—that our relationship was more important than proving she was right. If Joseph's techniques could teach me how to do this by choice, I'd be way ahead of the game with Charles, my nemesis at work.

"I'm willing to give it a try," I told Joseph. "Where do I begin?"

"You begin with the questions you ask yourself, with the realization that the kinds of questions you ask literally put you either in Learner or Judger mode. And we're most effective at virtually everything we do when we're in Learner. That's when we're most resourceful and flexible and have the most options.

"But don't worry if you take the Judger path every once in a while. That's just human. As your observer self gets stronger and more dependable, you'll find it increasingly easy to switch your questions and get back in Learner. That's where things open up again and you go toward the results you're seeking."

"You make it sound so easy," I said.

"It's easier than you think," Joseph said, "because everything you need is already built in. Continually asking Switching questions is what helps us to build a resilient observer and a robust Learner mindset. And along the way you're building your immunity to Judger mindset.

> Continually asking Switching questions is what helps us to build a resilient observer and a robust Learner mindset. And along the way you're building your immunity to Judger mindset.

"The signals for catching yourself in Judger are difficult to argue with, since they're your body's reactions and your moods. Remember what happened to me with the superintendent? The clues that I was in Judger were in my own moods and attitudes, which I've learned to associate with Judger—*self-righteousness, arrogance, superiority,* and *defensiveness.*

For example, you might be thinking, *I sure showed that guy!* Or, *Maybe that'll teach him to listen to me next time.* Or, *what an idiot that so-and-so is!* I've learned that any time I get into negative moods, Judger questions and attitudes are involved. Once I observe this state in myself I can change my questions and turn things around pretty easily, for a very different result."

He paused for a moment, then said, "Let's do an experiment. This is a way for you to actually experience what I'm talking about, so that you'll have more than just an intellectual understanding of the power of questions and mindsets. I'm going to recite two different sets of questions. As I do, notice how each set of questions affects you. Pay attention to your breathing, your muscles, your posture, and what you're feeling in different areas of your body. " He got up and walked over to the Choice Map. "Ask yourself these questions:

Whose fault is it?

What's wrong with me?

Why am I such a failure?

Why can't I ever do anything right?

Why is everybody so stupid and frustrating?

Haven't we already been there, done that?

Why bother?"

As he recited these questions, my chest tightened up. My shoulders stiffened. I was clutching up like a rookie pitcher in the last inning of an important game. I laughed uncomfortably, "Yeah, I definitely feel some tension here and there."

"Okay. How would you describe how you feel?"

I shrugged. "To be honest," I said. "I feel like that guy in the Judger Pit." I grappled for words to describe what I was feeling. Finally I came up with: *Hopeless and helpless. Pessimistic. Negative. Depleted. Depressed. Uptight. Victim. Loser.* I was relieved Joseph didn't insist I share everything going on with me.

"Now give yourself a moment or two to breathe and just observe whatever is going on with you right now. Imagine you're an observer watching yourself sitting here in my

Learner/Judger Questions*	
Judger	**Learner**
What's wrong with me?	What do I value about myself?
What's wrong with him/her?	What do I appreciate about him/her?
Whose fault is it?	Am I being responsible?
How can I prove I'm right?	What can I learn? What's useful?
Why is he/she so clueless and frustrating?	What is he/she thinking, feeling, and wanting?
Haven't we been there, done that?	What are the best steps forward?
Why bother?	What's possible?

*Each of us asks ourselves and others questions from both mindsets. With awareness, we have the capacity to choose at any moment which questions will frame our thinking, listening, speaking, and relating.

office. As you do this also notice if any feelings and sensations start to shift."

I did what he said. The changes were subtle at first.
It seemed like those negative sensations were starting to
diminish. I nodded. "Yes. I like that," I said.

"That's just a taste of the power of self-coaching and
how the observer self serves that process," Joseph said.
"Later on, we'll explore more tools for strengthening your
observer self. You'll be able to zero in on the kinds of questions that get you stuck and craft new questions that launch
you right into Learner territory. A friend of mine had a very
clever way of saying this: 'Either you have your questions,
or your questions have you.'"

> Either you have your questions, or
> your questions have you.

Joseph strode easily around the room, stroking his chin
as if he were considering something. Finally he stopped
and faced me again. "How about checking out the Learner
path," he asked. "Again, listen to the questions as if you were
asking them of yourself:

What happened?

What do I want?

What's useful about this?

What can I learn?

What's the other person thinking, feeling, and wanting?

What are my choices?

What's best to do now?

What's possible?"

With these questions I experienced a quiet excitement, very different from what I'd experienced with the Judger questions. My breathing got easier. My mood got lighter. I suddenly had more energy. I sensed a willingness and openness I certainly hadn't felt with the first set of questions. My shoulders relaxed. I hadn't felt this good in quite a while!

"What are some words you'd use to describe your experience now?" he asked.

I took a deep, easy breath. "Open. Lighter. Upbeat. Curious. Energetic. Optimistic." I chuckled. "I'm a damnsight more hopeful than I felt this morning . . . maybe there are solutions to my problems after all."

"Good," Joseph said. "Those feelings signal that you've stepped into Learner mindset. You're on the Learner path."

I heaved a sigh of relief. Even if I wasn't totally sold on everything Joseph was saying, maybe there was something to this coaching after all. I had to admit I was feeling more hopeful than I'd felt in a long time. Could it be that this guy actually was as good as Alexa seemed to believe he was? In spite of that big question mark on his business card, maybe he did have tools that could make a difference for me . . . as nutty as that might seem.

CHAPTER 4

We're All
Recovering Judgers

There is a crucial difference between being
caught up in a feeling and becoming aware
that you are being swept away by it. Socrates'
injunction "know thyself" speaks to this keystone
of emotional intelligence: awareness of
one's own feelings as they occur.

Daniel Goleman[11]

We took a short break while Joseph went off to get us
fresh coffee from the kitchenette adjacent to his office. He
was gone long enough for me to check my phone for texts
and voice messages. There was a voice message from Grace.
It was about her young assistant, Jennifer, who had messed
up on yet another assignment. "I've just got to vent," Grace
was saying. "I feel like I'm two seconds from firing her. Can
you call me right back?" I clicked off my phone. *Why was
Grace bothering me at work? Couldn't she handle Jennifer by
herself? Did she think I needed her problems on top of mine?*
My jaw and shoulders clenched up.

Just then Joseph returned with a tray that held two full
coffee mugs and containers of cream and sugar. I took a
mug and some cream, glad to focus on stirring what was in
my cup. I needed to settle myself down so I could listen to

what Joseph was starting to tell me. He was back to his story about the superintendent.

"My client and I both had a breakthrough that day," he was saying, "right after I recognized I had gotten hijacked by Judger."

"Wait a second," I said. "You used that term before— *getting hijacked by Judger*. What's a Judger highjack?"

"It's when something happens that triggers you, pushes your buttons" Joseph said. "You're going along with all the best intentions and you feel yourself tensing up, going Judger, and pretty soon you're not listening. You're getting increasingly defensive or you just want to run out of the room screaming."

"I know the feeling," I said. "I know it only too well. But isn't that pretty normal?"

"Normal, yes," Joseph said. "The problem is that normal or not, if we want to get things accomplished, we've got to have a tool for switching into Learner mindset. Once we've done that our perspective will change and open up. That's how you recover from a Judger hijack."

"That's all well and good," I said. "But did you ever get through to that guy? Did he ever *get* it?" The minute I asked that question I realized I'd been asking those same questions about myself: *Did I get it?* Something about that superintendent's story was making me uneasy. But what was it?

"Oh, sure. The superintendent eventually got it," Joseph said. "In the end, he made an interesting comment. With the

'Judger agenda,' as he called it, 'the costs can be tremendous. The future can be only a recycled version of the past. And with the Learner program the power is on. The juice is flowing. You can actually make a new future for yourself!'"

> With Judger mindset, the costs can be tremendous. The future can be only a recycled version of the past. And with the Learner program the power is on.
> The juice is flowing. You can actually make a new future for yourself.

Suddenly I knew what was bugging me. That story about the superintendent could actually be about *me*.

"You make it sound like any kind of judgment is a bad thing," I interrupted. "But I disagree. I could never do my job without making judgments . . . and I take a lot of pride in making good judgments. You have to judge when you're making technological choices, or when you're choosing a vendor to buy from, or whether you're assigning the best person to do a certain job."

"By all means," Joseph said. "You bring up an important point. Exercising judgment is about making good choices. I call that *discernment*, or *acuity*, which is essential in a job like yours. So I'm not talking about judgment in that sense of the word. I'm talking about *being judgmental*, as in fault-finding or dwelling on the negative or being critical. Judger and judgment are two very different things.

"In fact, Judger mindset is the enemy of good judgment. When we're judgmental, brain activity gets spikey; the big muscles of our bodies prepare themselves for fighting or running. In some cases we freeze; our brains just shut down, and it becomes difficult to think at all. It's the classic fight-or-flight response, with all our energies going in the direction of running away, putting up a good fight . . . or shutting down in resignation or defeat. Those are all variations of our survival mode responses. Using good judgment is the opposite of all this. It's a shame those words—judgment and judgmental—even sound alike. One of my dictionaries defines judgment*al* as 'attacking self or others.' Nothing could be more different from *exercising good judgment.*"

> Judger mindset is the enemy
> of good judgment.

"So Judger always means judgmental," I said.

"That's right," Joseph said, taking a sip of coffee, "Judger is always judgmental. What's more, Judger has two faces—either we're being judgmental toward *ourselves* or we're being judgmental toward *other people.*"

I fell silent, trying to absorb what he was telling me. How did it apply to me? I'd certainly gotten judgmental when I listened to Grace's message. I'd jumped right into Judger. But Grace calling me at work about Jennifer wasn't exactly using the best judgment on Grace's part, either. Or was I being judgmental about her, too?

Joseph settled back into his chair. "What's going through your mind right now?" he asked.

"I can't deny that I've been spending a lot of time in Judger lately," I began hesitantly. "But how do you avoid going down that path when you've got a guy like Charles to deal with? He's the main source of the problems with our team and with our miserable results. He's driving me nuts." I clamped my jaw shut, not wanting to say anything more. I didn't like thinking about myself as being so much in Judger. In fact, I was really starting to resent this Judger stuff. Besides, how do you stay on the Learner path with problems piling up all around you?

Joseph must have read my mind because the next thing he said was, "Remember that slipping into Judger is just part of being human, especially when things aren't going well. In this respect, we're all recovering Judgers. No doubt about it, our Judger nature can be a bit addictive. And the more we indulge it the more it becomes a habit and takes over. While it's true we can never get rid of Judger, we *can* learn to manage it, to just be with it. Once you can do that a whole new way of being becomes available to you. Awareness, commitment, compassion, courage, forgiveness, acceptance—with a dash of humor—that's what it takes to keep recovering ourselves and resetting our course back to the Learner path.

"The whole idea is to accept Judger and practice Learner, moment by moment by moment. This work is not about getting on the Learner path and staying there. That's a pipe dream. Real personal power depends on how good we get at recovering from Judger once it takes over. That's why I got such a kick out of that situation with my superintendent client. Sure I got hijacked by Judger, but the instant I realized it, I could rescue myself and get back on the Learner path. Sometimes it's even fun to see how fast I can catch Judger and how fast I can recover.

"Frankly," Joseph said with a smile, "sometimes I find myself slipping into Judger several times an hour! By the way, in your workbook you'll find a tool called *Make Friends with Judger*."

Accept Judger and practice Learner— moment by moment by moment.

The idea of having to deal with Judger forever didn't please me very much. On the other hand, at least it meant I wasn't any worse off than anyone else.

Joseph paused for a moment, then said, "Tell me more about Charles."

"He's second in command on the project team I head up," I said, hoping my exasperation didn't show too much. "But this guy challenges everything I say. I must admit, he's probably got a legitimate bone to pick with me. He was passed over for the position I got, and boy, does he resent it. I would, too, if I were in his shoes! He's a real know-it-all, picky and petty. He's out to sabotage me. That's the bottom line. And it looks like he's succeeding."

"When you think about Charles, what's the first question that pops into your mind?"

I chuckled. "That's easy! *How can I put a leash on this guy before he destroys me?*"

"Anything else?"

"Lots of things! *How can I stay in control? Aren't I supposed to be the one who's the leader of this team? How can I make this guy get with the program?*"

"And?"

"*How did I ever get myself into this mess? Whatever made me think I could handle being a leader?*" I paused for a moment, then asserted, "Listen, the thing is, Charles needs to change as much as you seem to think I do."

"What you're saying about Charles may be true," Joseph said. "But you're the one in my office now. Change begins with the person who wants the change. Right?"

That really knocked the wind out of my sails. I sat back in my chair and took a deep breath. "What am I supposed to do, ignore the fact that he stabs me in the back every chance he gets?" I was getting steamed. "There's no way to separate my reactions from what Charles does!"

Change begins with the person who wants the change.

"Ah, but that's the beauty of it," Joseph said. "You *can* separate your reactions from his behavior—and anyone else's. Until you do, you'll keep giving away your power. You'll be just like a puppet, with no control of your own. Anybody, including Charles, will be able to pull your strings and hijack your Judger. It's a matter of whether you have your Judger or your Judger has you."

Either you have your Judger or your Judger has you.

"I'm not agreeing or disagreeing with you," I said, secretly seething inside. "I don't think I could possibly see this situation with Charles any differently."

"Is that a question?" Joseph asked.

"What are you saying?"

"Can you reshape that statement as a question?"

"You mean, like, *How else can I think about this?*" To my surprise, the moment I asked myself this question I felt a subtle shift inside. For one thing, I let go of the breath I hadn't even known I was holding, and my shoulders relaxed enough that Joseph probably saw it.

"Exactly. Did you notice? You just switched yourself into Learner. Quick as that. And here's my answer: No matter what Charles or anyone else might do, you can use the Choice Map, and what you're learning about your body's messages, to identify when you've gone into Judger. Those messages will remind you to stand back and observe where you are. You will have empowered your observer self, so you can watch your own movie for a moment. Then you'll be able to tell the difference between what Charles does and *what you choose to do with what he does.*"

I tried to take in Joseph's lesson. It wasn't easy. Judger questions were still running through my brain. I guess Judger had a grip on me where Charles was concerned. Was that true in my marriage, too?

"Let's go back for a moment to that figure standing at the crossroads," Joseph said, tapping his finger on the Start arrow of the Choice Map. "Remember, this figure represents every one of us at the moment when we're hit with something and we have to deal with it. We're stumped. Regardless of the situation, it's vital to remember we have choice about how to respond. Do you know what those choices are?"

"We can just react and jump right into Judger," I said, feeling my way along, "Or we can pause, check in with our moods and body feelings, and notice what kinds of Self-Q's we're asking, then try to choose Learner. We can choose . . . we have choice."

Fireworks started going off in my mind. *I actually do have choice! And I can choose Learner when I want to.* Maybe Joseph's tools really could make a difference with my results at work.

"I have to say," I told him cautiously, "maybe it's not as difficult to distinguish between Judger and Learner as I thought."

Joseph actually clapped his hands. "Yes. Yes, that's great! Once you're able to observe your own thoughts and feelings, and recognize the differences between Learner and Judger, you step into self-coaching territory, where you grab hold of the power of choice." Joseph seemed tremendously excited by this notion. "You're a quick study," he exclaimed. "I see another of the traits Alexa values in you so much." He glanced at his wristwatch. "We've been talking for a long time. Let's stop here for the day."

Joseph opened a drawer in his desk and took out some colorful copies of the Choice Map.

"Take these with you," he said, handing them to me. "Study the Choice Map when you get to your office. And take one home to post on your refrigerator."

I groaned inwardly. What on earth would I tell Grace about all this! She'd want to know where I'd gotten the Choice Map and why I'd put it on the refrigerator.

"This map illustrates fundamental distinctions between Learner and Judger mindsets," Joseph said, as we walked down the hall. "Ultimately, the message is pretty simple. Change your questions, change your *results*. This is core self-management know-how for every recovering Judger." He smiled and added: "Remember, Ben, that's *all* of us, we're all recovering Judgers."

Change your questions, change your *results*.

At the doors of his outer office, Joseph stopped and turned to face me. Over his shoulder, on the wall with the Question Thinking Hall of Fame, I spotted a picture of Alexa. It appeared to be from a major magazine, profiling her for some award. Embarrassed though I was to admit it, I hadn't known about this article or her award. Given how long I'd known Alexa I certainly should have.

"See you next time," Joseph said, shaking my hand warmly.

My head was spinning. My whole life was being turned upside down. What really puzzled me was that I also felt lighter, more optimistic than I'd been in ages. One thing Alexa was right about—this Joseph guy had a provocative way of looking at how to make changes in our lives. I began to imagine that maybe, by working with him, I'd come up with answers—or was it new questions—that could put my career back on track.

CHAPTER 5

Kitchen Talk

The big question is whether you are going
to be able to say a hearty "yes" to your adventure.

Joseph Campbell

It was early in the morning when Grace found the Choice
Map I had stuck on the refrigerator door the night before.
As usual, I awoke to the smell of fresh coffee and made my
way downstairs to the kitchen. Grace is always up before
me. She's one of those people who wakes up cheerful and
enthusiastic about each new day. I'm just the opposite, and
I know it sometimes puts Grace on edge. She claims that I'm
like a bear coming out of hibernation in the morning. I don't
think I'm quite that bad, but I don't exactly start the day off
with a song in my heart.

As I entered the kitchen, I found Grace standing in front
of the refrigerator with her back to me. She appeared to be
engrossed with the Choice Map. I was immediately worried
about what she might to say. I was pretty sure she'd start
probing, and I'd have to tell her the whole thing—about
my trouble at work and all the rest of it. That would lead to

how I'd gotten the Choice Map and why I'd posted it on the refrigerator. Then I might have to tell her about why Alexa had referred me to Joseph, and that could turn into an emotional minefield.

While I was worrying about how I would avoid telling her the whole story, Grace suddenly turned around and gave me a big hug.

"Where did you get this?" she asked. "It's terrific!"

She took the Choice Map off the refrigerator door and started waving it around in her hand. I mumbled something about it being a handout for a special training at work, and then poured a cup of coffee for myself and one for Grace.

"I'm amazed," she said. "I've already learned something from this. You remember that message I left you about Jennifer, my assistant at work? I guess I've been riding her pretty hard lately. I can just feel her cringing any time I get within a few feet of her. Looking at the Choice Map, I realize I've been a real Judger with her, like it says here, and I'm sure that's put her on edge. She's been messing up a lot, but this makes me wonder if I've been contributing to the problem. After all, nobody does their best work when their boss is expecting the worst from them."

"It's all in the kinds of questions you ask." I didn't even think before the words just popped out of my mouth.

"What questions?" Grace asked. "I don't ever get that far with poor Jennifer."

"According to this guy Joseph, who gave me this map . . ."

"Wait," Grace interrupted. "Who's Joseph?"

I stared at her blankly for a moment, debating about whether to tell her the truth. I decided to keep things simple. "He's this consultant Alexa hired," I told her, determined not to go into any more details than absolutely necessary. Yesterday, right after meeting with Joseph, I'd spent an hour studying the map, preparing answers for any questions Grace might have. "He claims that most of the time we're not even aware of the questions we ask ourselves or other people. That's what the Choice Map teaches. It's a reminder to look carefully at those questions, because they affect how we think, feel, and act and even how other people respond to us."

Grace looked puzzled. I pressed close to her and pointed to the little guy at the crossroads. "There's the key right there," I said, pointing to the words *Thoughts, Feelings, Circumstances* near the figure's head. "The moment anything happens to us, that's when we start asking ourselves questions. The sooner we recognize what we're asking, the better. That way we have more options." *Was this really me talking?* I was amazed at how much I recalled of Joseph's teachings. The more we talked, the more comfortable I was getting with this QT stuff.

"The main thing I see are these two paths," Grace said, tracing first one and then the other with her finger. "Take the Learner route and you'll move right along. The Learner guy is saying, 'What do I want? What are my choices?' This other one is asking, 'What can I learn?' Oh, you're right, these are all questions. And the guy on the Judger path, he's all caught up with different questions like: *'Whose fault is it? What's wrong with them?'* I'll tell you, Ben, at the office, every time I hear a pin drop or somebody sigh, the first thing that pops into my head is, *'Oh, Lord, what's wrong now? What else can Jennifer possibly mess up?'* And then, in a flash, I'm down on her. Do you know what she did yesterday, Ben? She . . . oh, hold it. That's taking me right into Judger territory, isn't it?"

"The way it works," I explained, "is that from moment to moment, stuff happens. Good stuff and bad stuff. It sort of hits us unawares. Then, especially if we have a strong Judger habit, our questions tend to follow that same pattern. If we're more in Learner mode, we'll ask questions in that direction."

"Action follows thought," Grace added. "It's a basic principle. But I never thought about it in terms of questions. *Action follows questions.* Seems to me the trick is to just keep ourselves in a Learner frame of mind."

"According to Joseph," I told Grace, "nobody stays in Learner all the time. It's natural to slip into Judger now and then. In fact, we alternate between the two mindsets all the time. It's just human nature." Even as I said those words, I was thinking about the argument she and I got into that day I dropped her off at the airport. I was still feeling embarrassed about how I'd treated her. I wasn't ready to go into all that with Grace, but at least I summoned up the nerve to mention part of it.

"It's so easy to go into Judger," I said, carefully choosing my words. "For example, the other day I was trying to pull out into traffic and nearly got hit by a taxi that was going about twice the speed it should have. I instantly went into Judger. It was like a bolt of lightning, you know? It happened that fast. In an instant, I was ready to punch the guy out."

"Sometimes you really worry me," Grace said, shaking her head.

My shoulders tensed up and I could feel myself getting defensive. I knew she didn't approve of my driving habits, though I'd never had an accident. We'd gotten into arguments about this before, but this time a part of me stopped and said, *Don't go there, buddy.* I took a deep breath, shrugged my shoulders, and just tried to keep things easy and relaxed.

"It's just an example. What I now see, thanks to Joseph's Choice Map, is how that close call immediately put me in Judger. I'm not saying I handled it well. In fact, I know I didn't, because I was angry as hell for the next couple of hours. I was experiencing what Joseph calls a Judger hijack."

I really wanted to tell Grace the whole story, about how I'd lumped together everything I'd been experiencing lately. I'd been stewing about whether or not to resign. I was irritated about having to meet with Joseph. I was hurt, worried about my whole career going up in smoke, and angry with

Grace for pressuring me about our relationship in the midst of all this. My life had become just one big . . . well, one big Judger Pit, I guess, and I had been sinking in the mud.

I tensed all over as I realized I'd been as much of a challenge to Joseph as that judgmental superintendent he'd told me about. That first day I'd slouched into his office certain that meeting with him was going to be a hopeless waste of my time. In the mood I'd been in, it was a miracle anything he said had gotten through to me. Now I was telling Grace about Joseph's ideas as if I actually knew what I was talking about!

"I'm thinking this map is a good reminder of what happens to me when I get stuck in one of my Judger heads," Grace said. She turned away for a moment and sat down at the breakfast table. She sipped her coffee and nibbled her toast as she studied the map. I continued standing, leaning against the counter, watching her. After a moment, Grace looked up a little shyly.

"Maybe this could help us . . . you know, in our relationship," she said. "What do you think?" There was not the slightest hint of blame or judgment in her voice. I was really grateful for that.

"Joseph says that life is filled with those moments when something hits us and sets us off on one path or another. . . ."

"But what do *you* think," Grace asked, "I mean, about it helping *us*—you and me?"

This time I thought I detected a bit of an edge in her voice. She really wanted me to tell her exactly what I was thinking. "As I said," I answered. "I think it applies well to any and all areas of our lives. We can all use better tools."

"What's that supposed to mean, better tools?" she asked, sounding definitely irritated.

I tried to ignore Grace's eyes. So far our conversation had gone so well, I didn't want it to turn sour. I was already asking myself: *What stupid thing did I say to mess things up again? And why did she bring up our relationship in the first place? Talk about bad timing!* And then I caught myself. Those simple little questions were pushing me right down the Judger path. This time, though, I saw it coming. I imagined Joseph as a coach on the sidelines shouting to me, *Learner! Learner! Remember the Choice Map! Change your questions! You can turn this around!* Almost instantly a new question occurred to me: *How can I keep things positive between Grace and me?*

"Sorry," Grace was saying. "I just realized I was starting to go Judger on you."

For a moment I felt puzzled, then relieved as it dawned on me what had happened. Grace had started going down the Judger path. We both had. And then she stopped herself, and so did I. *Amazing!* In spite of myself, I smiled.

"What are you smiling about?" Grace asked. She got up from the table, took her dishes to the sink, then turned to face me.

"Sweetheart," I said. "You're wonderful!" I took her in my arms and held her close. She stiffened but quickly softened and hugged me back.

"Do you remember that night when we had dinner at the Metropol and I was late?" I asked. I felt her nodding her head against my shoulder.

"We really got into it, didn't we, about who got their times mixed up? Then you did a remarkable thing. You suddenly just dropped the whole argument, and everything shifted. We got connected again. Do you remember?"

"Mm hmm, I sure do!" She chuckled, planting a kiss on my cheek.

It was difficult being serious while remembering that night, but I really wanted to get my point across. "Joseph talks about switching from Judger to Learner, and how we can do that with a single question."

"Like when I ask myself: *Do I want to win this argument?* Or, *Do I want to have a good time?*" Grace drew away from me but kept her hands on my shoulders.

"Is that how you do your magic?" I asked.

"Some of it," she said, leaning into me again. "But I never thought of it in terms of questions."

"I'm serious," I said, wanting to make certain I got my point across. "I just realized that you're a natural at the very thing Joseph teaches. I'll bet you do it by changing your questions, even if you're not aware of it. You take yourself straight to Learner. That's how you shift your mood!"

"I like those shifts!"

"Me, too," I said, hugging her again. I still wanted to

know more about how she made those shifts. "How did you learn to do that?"

Before she could answer, the alarm chirped on her phone. Grace always sets it to alert her when it's time to get ready for work.

"Oh, no!" She sighed, suddenly all businesslike. "I'm sorry, Ben. I'd love to call in late but I really can't. I have an important meeting this morning."

In the next instant, she was dashing up the stairs to finish getting ready. Twenty minutes later she kissed me goodbye and raced out the door. When I got around to pouring myself another cup of coffee, I glanced at the refrigerator and realized the Choice Map was gone. Grace had taken it to work with her!

As I was getting in my car to leave for the office, I noticed a piece of paper stuck under the windshield wiper. It was a hurriedly written note from Grace:

Darling,

Thank you so much for the Choice Map—and especially for the good talk this morning. You can't imagine how much it means to me!

Love,

Grace

I'd never expected Grace to take the Choice Map. I felt great about the note. Clearly she liked Joseph's ideas. At least for now, I'd redeemed myself in her eyes. Good! That was one less pressure in my life.

CHAPTER 6

Switching Questions

Between stimulus and response, there is a space.
In that space is our power to choose
our response. In our response
lies our growth and our freedom.

Viktor Frankl

As I stepped off the elevator at the Pearl Building, I found Joseph watering his ficus trees with a large red watering can. It surprised me to see him doing something I would have handed off to my staff. He turned to me with a friendly smile. "I love having plants around. It's a daily reminder that all living things require our attention," he said. "No office should be without at least a plant or two. My wife, Sarah, is the gardener in our family. She says plants force you to ask yourself questions. Are they getting enough water, enough sun? Do they need a little pruning? Do they need special nutrients? They thrive on questions, just as we humans do." He quickly finished his gardening chores and we went inside.

"When we finished our last meeting, we were talking about the Choice Map and what it tells us about Learner and Judger mindsets," Joseph began. "Have you had any further thoughts about any of this?"

I guardedly told him about Grace, our talk in the kitchen, and how she'd taken the Choice Map from the refrigerator to work with her.

"It's clear that we get different results depending on which of the two paths we take—Learner or Judger," I told Joseph hesitantly. "Maybe I get stuck in Judger more than I'd like to admit."

"Fortunately, there's a fast track out of Judger as soon as you recognize that mindset has you in its grip." Joseph pointed to the little road in the middle of the map, joining the Judger and the Learner path. A sign labeled it the *Switching Lane*. "That lane is the key to change. Once you notice you're in Judger—I mean nonjudgmentally, of course—you get to Learner by asking Switching questions. Let's look at how that works.

"When you're standing in Judger," Joseph continued, "the whole world usually looks pretty bleak. Even though the world is actually filled with infinite possibilities, we have only limited access to noticing them when seeing with Judger eyes or listening with Judger ears. Let me show you how to change your viewpoint, how to literally see and hear everything differently, sometimes almost immediately. For a moment, locate yourself on the Judger Path, right where the Switching Lane begins."

I turned my attention to the map and focused on the juncture of the Judger path and the Switching Lane.

"Any time you step onto this path," he continued, pointing to the Switching Lane, " you automatically step into choice.

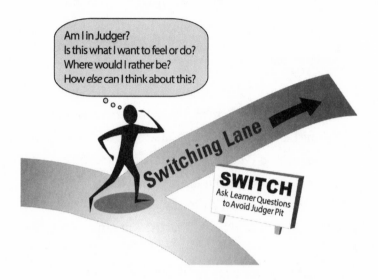

You wake up. You uncover a whole new view of the world. You literally switch how you're thinking about what's possible. When you observe your own thoughts, especially Judger ones, they relax their grip on you, and you increase your ability to choose freely what to think and do next.

"You're talking about choice like it's something we possess . . . a capacity."

"Absolutely! We're all born with that capacity," Joseph exclaimed. "That's what makes us human. Choice is always ours, although it takes practice, and sometimes courage, to make the best use of it. The author Viktor Frankl spoke of 'the last of human freedoms—to choose one's attitude in any given circumstances, to choose one's own way.'

"And making this practical is what it's all about. That's where the rubber hits the road. Whenever you sense you might be in Judger, pause, take a deep breath, get curious, and ask yourself, *Am I in Judger?* Of course, the tricky part is that you have to ask that question nonjudgmentally! If the answer is *Yes, I am in Judger*, you can step onto the Switching Lane by asking simple questions like: *Do I want to be in Judger?* And *Where would I like to be?*" Joseph laughed. "Is it easy? Not always, but it *is* simple. The Switching Lane takes you to the Learner path. You'll find a list of Switching questions in your workbook. That list is another of the tools in the QT system."

Something was nagging at the back of my mind, but I couldn't quite get hold of it. Then it dawned on me. I remembered asking Grace how she shifted her moods so quickly. I realized she used Switching questions, whether she was aware of it or not.

Joseph was gazing thoughtfully out the window. "Let me tell you a story that illustrates how Switching questions can make a huge difference in performance and results. It's a true story about my daughter Kelly, who's an avid gymnast. In college, she was even training for a national championship competition.

"Here's what happened. During training Kelly would perform quite well most of the time, but only *most* of the time. Sarah and I knew she'd never make the team that way. She had the ability, but her performance was too erratic.

"So, on her request, we worked with Kelly so she could make the improvement she needed to make the team. First, we asked her what she thought about just before a performance. She discovered that in those crucial moments she always asked just one basic question, *Will I fall this time?*"

"Which is a Judger question," I observed.

"Right," Joseph said, "because it focuses her attention on falling and failing. And asking it led to what my daughter calls *Judger trouble*. That question really interfered with her performance. So the three of us worked on finding a Switching question she could ask herself to propel her quickly into Learner. The new question was Kelly's own idea: *How can I do a great job?* That did the trick. Using that new question, she reprogrammed herself by directing her attention in a positive direction. Her performance improved exponentially and also became highly predictable. Kelly says that new question helps her stay *in the zone.*"

"Did she make the team?"

"She sure did," Joseph said. "And, by the way, she came home with a trophy. It wasn't first place, but I was really proud. I have to confess that 20 years ago, I would have probably chastised her for not taking first place. Oh, I tell you, having children teaches us to ask a whole new set of questions! By the way, you'll find Kelly's story in my Question Thinking Hall of Fame."

"This all sounds like a bit of magic, to me," I quipped. "Or a miracle."

"It's neither magic nor a miracle," Joseph replied, smiling. "It's a *method*. With questions we can even change ourselves physiologically. For example, the worried question *What if I get fired?* can set off a whole chain of biochemical stress reactions in your body. Kelly's question *Will I fall this time?* reminded her of past failures and made her anxious, which interfered with her performance and reinforced any old programming for failure. Consciously, of course, she didn't want to fail, but that's exactly what happened anyway with that old question. *Thought sets intention.* Learner questions program us with a positive intention—in Kelly's case, for the right attitude—and moves for an outstanding performance."

"By implication you're suggesting that Judgers can't be top performers," I reflected. "I can't agree with you there. I've known Judger types who produced quite a lot."

"Be careful about using labels like 'Judger types.' There isn't anybody who's a Judger person or a Learner person. These terms refer only to mindsets and, as you know by now, every one of us has both mindsets and always will. That's the conundrum of being human. Labels are just too handy, and that makes them sticky like self-adhesive stamps. On the other hand, our mindsets are dynamic; they can change from moment to moment. The point is that Question Thinking makes us aware of our mindsets and puts us more in charge of making the changes we want. And that's something we can begin at any moment.

"At the same time, you are absolutely right that many people spend more time in Judger than Learner," Joseph said. "And they may be quite driven and productive. However, their success often comes with very high costs. People with an overactive Judger can drive themselves and everyone around them nuts, and eventually that lowers productivity, cooperation, and creativity. Not to mention morale! It's hard to feel loyal to or trust someone who lives in high Judger most of the time. Having an overactive Judger can build resentment and conflict, whether with your family or your colleagues.

"If you want people to be really engaged and involved, Learner is the path to take. An organization led by people in high Judger tends to have greater levels of stress, conflict, and people problems. Those kinds of leaders are not well equipped to be flexible and adaptable—or successful—in meeting challenges. And just imagine the havoc that Judger plays when you take that mindset home with you at night!

"My wife, Sarah, once wrote an article exploring the difference between high Judger marriages and high Learner marriages. Her premise was that our experience of intimate relationships will be very different depending on whether we look on our partner with Learner eyes or Judger eyes. Sarah points out that with Learner eyes we're able to focus on what we appreciate about the other person and what's working in our relationship, at least most of the time. We build from strengths rather than dwelling on flaws—our own or our partner's."

I nodded, thinking that this made sense.

"When we're in Judger, whether at home or work, everything can seem like a roadblock, and always somebody else's fault. There's no power there. When that happens we need to go back to basic Switching questions, like: *Am I in Judger? Will it get me what I really want? Where would I rather be? What am I responsible for here?* Pause, take a deep breath, put yourself on the Switching Lane and you can step right onto the Learner path."

"If what you say is true, I could just stay in Learner by always keeping those questions in mind."

"Theoretically, yes. But life really isn't that simple. And not one of us is a saint. We're all going to fall into Judger from time to time—that's the point I'm emphasizing when I say we're all recovering Judgers," Joseph continued. "But I promise you this—the more you take to heart the Choice Map and Switching questions, the faster you'll be able to step into Learner, the easier it will be, and the longer you'll be able to stay there. You'll also spend less time in Judger, and the experience itself is usually less intense, so the consequences of being there will be minimized.

"And remember," Joseph continued, "Judger has two faces, one being judgmental toward ourselves, the other being judgmental toward others. The results can look quite different, but they come from that same judgmental, critical place in our thinking.

"If we focus our Judger mindset on ourselves, for

example, with questions such as: *Why am I such a failure?* we hurt our self-confidence and may even feel depressed. On the other hand, when we focus our Judger mindset on others, with questions such as: *Why is everyone around me so stupid and frustrating?* we tend to get angry, resentful, and hostile. Either way, with Judger, we usually end up in some kind of conflict either with ourselves or with others. When Judger takes control it's impossible to find genuine connection, resolution, or any sense of peace. That's why many mediators use the Learner/Judger mindset material with their clients, especially the Choice Map.

"Let me give you an example of Judger when we aim it at ourselves. Years ago, Sarah was talking with Ruth, her editor at one of the magazines she writes for. They were sharing how they had both had issues with managing their weight. Sarah told Ruth how she used the Choice Map to help her feel calmer, be kinder to herself, and make better choices about eating. Ruth got so excited that she asked Sarah to write an article about her experiences.

"In the article, Sarah described how the questions people typically ask themselves about eating either get them in trouble with their weight, self-image, and self-confidence or help them to be successful and content with themselves. The troublemaker questions she listed included: *What's wrong with me? Why am I out of control again? Why am I such a hopeless glutton?*"

"Those are all judgmental questions," I interjected.

"Right. And whenever Sarah started down the Judger Path with questions like those, she really beat herself up, which of course sent her spiraling right down to the Judger Pit. Unfortunately, those Judger meltdowns usually caused her to feel out of control and eat even more. Sometimes that led to real bingeing. Once Sarah recognized the impact those troublemaker Judger questions had on her, she decided to look for Switching questions to rescue herself. She said that Switching questions are the best thing she's ever found for getting back in control. Her new questions included: *What's really going on with me? Am I willing to forgive myself?* And *how do I want to feel?*"

"Which got her onto the Switching Lane, her shortcut back to Learner," I said.

"Right again. Once she switched into Learner, she figured out some questions to help her stay there whenever she felt herself going Judger: *What will serve me best right now? Am I being honest with myself? What do I really need? What can I do to feel better that doesn't involve eating?* Whenever she asked herself one of these questions she felt empowered rather than out of control. Not only that, she's gotten herself in great shape. She tells me it's pretty easy to maintain now."

Judging by the photos of Sarah on Joseph's desk, I certainly didn't think Sarah looked like a woman with weight issues. But all this talk was making me even more uncomfortably aware of how often the questions I asked myself were straight out of Judger mindset.

"From what I've seen so far," Joseph said, in a surprisingly accepting tone of voice, "while you obviously don't have trouble with your weight, you still have a lot of self-Judger going on."

"I can't disagree," I hedged. "But what's your basis for saying that?"

"That's easy," Joseph said. "Do you remember that time you were so sure I saw you as a Judger *and* a loser?"

"Yes," I said, hesitantly, sensing I was stepping into something I would regret.

"That's the perspective that keeps you bogged down and resigned about being able to change. But while you aim judgmental questions at yourself," Joseph said, looking straight at me, "you're also pretty good at targeting other people."

"I agree I can be pretty hard on myself . . . and on other people." I began to squirm. "But sometimes people really are jerks and idiots. I know I'm right about that. You've got to accept this as a fact of life and exercise good common sense, or good judgment, as you already said."

Without comment, Joseph directed my attention back to the Choice Map. As I held it in my hand, he leaned forward and pointed at the figure that was starting down the Judger Path. Then he pointed to the thought bubble over his head. It contained just one question, which I read out loud: *Whose fault is it?*

What jumped into my mind were all the troubles I'd been having at work. I focused on that stark moment of truth when I concluded I was a failure and would have to resign. The shame I felt was just awful. Did Judger have a hand in shame, too? I was certainly in my Judger-head at that moment, having judged myself as a loser. But wasn't I justified? I couldn't deny I'd screwed up.

"What's going through your mind right now?"

I replied with discomfort, "The more we talk, the more I see I've got to accept the blame for a lot of what's happened."

"Blame," Joseph said. "Tell me exactly what that word means to you."

"The bottom line? It means I should step down. I'm the incompetent one here. Period! End of conversation."

"Back up for a moment. What happens when you change your question from 'Who's to *blame?*' to 'What am I *responsible* for?'"

Those questions did hit me differently but I couldn't figure out why. "Blame. Responsibility. Aren't they the same thing?"

"Not at all," Joseph said. "Blame is Judger. Responsibility is Learner. There's a world of difference between them. Focusing on blame blinds us from seeing real alternatives and solutions. It's almost impossible to fix a problem when operating from Judger blame. Blame can be paralyzing. Blame keeps us stuck in the past. Responsibility, on the other hand, paves the path for a better future. If you focus your questions on what you might be responsible for, you also open your mind to new possibilities. You're free to create alternatives that lead to positive change."

Blame keeps us stuck in the past.
Responsibility paves the path for a
better future.

Blame can be paralyzing? What did he mean by that? I felt an urge to get up, stretch, and walk around. I took a break, went to the bathroom, and splashed some cold water on my face. After I returned, Joseph said, "Remind me about what you said about Charles the other day."

Ah, back to Charles! Now I knew I was on solid ground. It would be easy to prove to Joseph how good judgment served me in this case, that my feelings about Charles were not just the product of Judger attitudes. "I told you, if it weren't for Charles I wouldn't be in such a mess," I said. "That's obvious. He's playing a win-lose game. You'd have to be blind not to see that."

Without replying, Joseph directed me to turn to my workbook and find the pages labeled *Learner/Judger Chart: Mindsets and Relationships*. I studied it for a moment, checking out the two columns that listed key characteristics of Learner and Judger. The content of those two columns was very different. It hit me immediately how one way of thinking would take me down the Judger path while the other would pull me up to Learner territory.

"This chart guides us to become much better observers of ourselves." Joseph said. "It lists Learner and Judger qualities and characteristics to help us to discern where we are at any moment. It's invaluable for helping us to strengthen our observer self and shift from Judger to Learner. Let's use it right now to do some exploring. Think about Charles. Then read off any words or phrases that leap to your attention."

"*Reactive and automatic. Know-it-all. Listening for agreement or disagreement. Self-righteous...*" I stopped. Everything I was reading was in the *Judger Mindset* column. My jaw tightened. Then I turned to the *Learner Mindset* column. Only one phrase caught my eye: *Values not-knowing*. I was puzzled.

"I'm not sure what you mean by *values not-knowing*," I said.

"It's like when someone is doing research," Joseph explained. "You want to discover something new, which is impossible if you're attached to the conviction that you already know all the answers. Valuing not-knowing is the basis of learning and all creativity and innovation. It's the state of mind that's open to all kinds of new possibilities and even hoping you might be surprised. Instead of defending old opinions or positions or answers, your goal is to look with fresh eyes. Remember Einstein's words: 'Learn from yesterday, live for today, hope for tomorrow. The important thing is to not stop questioning.' I like to think of this as 'rational humility,' a maturity we develop by admitting that it's impossible to ever have all the answers."

Rational humility! I liked that. That's how it felt when I was doing technological research. Beyond that, especially

Learner/Judger Mindset* Chart

Judger Mindset	Learner Mindset
Judgmental (of self/others/facts)	Accepting (of self/others/facts)
Reactive and automatic	Responsive and thoughtful
Critical and negative	Appreciative and has humility
Close-minded	Open-minded
Know-it-all, self-righteous	Comfortable with not knowing
Blame oriented	Responsibility oriented
Problem focused	Solution focused
Own point of view only	Takes multiple perspectives
Inflexible and rigid	Flexible/adaptive/creative
Either/or thinking	Both/and thinking
Defends assumptions	Questions assumptions
Mistakes are bad	Mistakes are to learn from
Presumes scarcity	Presumes sufficiency
Possibilities seen as limited	Possibilities seen as unlimited
Primary stance: protective	Primary stance: curious

Learner/Judger Relationships*

Judger Relating	Learner Relating
Win-lose relating	Win-win relating
Dismissive, demeaning	Accepting, empathizing
Advocacy	Inquiry
Separate from self/others	Connected with self/others
Fears differences	Values differences
Feedback considered rejection	Feedback considered worthwhile
Conversation: own agenda	Conversation: collaborative
Conflict: destructive	Conflict: constructive
"Judger ears" *listen for:*	"Learner ears" *listen for:*
Agree or disagree	Understanding and facts
What's wrong re: self and/or others	What's valuable re: self and/or others
Danger	Possibility
Seeks to attack or is defensive	Seeks to appreciate/resolve/create

*Both mindsets are normal; each of us has both and always will. With awareness, each of us has the capacity to choose where we relate from in any moment.

with relationships, I felt like I was in foreign territory. Suddenly, I was confused. *Was it Charles or I who was reactive and automatic? Was it Charles or I who was the know-it-all? Who was listening for agreement or disagreement? Who was self-righteous? Who was the big Judger here?*

Before I could recover from my confusion, Joseph hit me with a new question. "What do you think it costs you to spend so much time in the Judger Pit?"

"*Costs* me?" I said quietly, looking at Joseph and then at the floor. His question had hit me like a thunderbolt. "I don't even want to think about the cost to the company for my Judger habits. First of all, I'm getting a pretty good salary, but it's money down a black hole in terms of what I'm producing. On top of that, I'm starting to suspect that I've created a no-win situation that's brought my whole team down. I dread going to meetings with those people. And the trickle down to other departments we work with...well, this isn't a pretty picture!"

Joseph was nodding, apparently satisfied with my insights. "This is real progress," he told me. "You're doing great, Ben."

"Great? What are you talking about? This is a disaster. Throw me a lifeline, would you? How do I get out of this?"

"I *could* drag you out," Joseph said, "but I'm going to give you something even more valuable—tools to get yourself out. I'm a big believer in the 'teach 'em to fish' philosophy. Now, I want you to bring to mind a time when you were in Learner in a work situation. Got the picture? Recall as vividly as you can what that experience was like. If you have trouble remembering, take a look at the Learner side of the chart."

Right away I recalled my best work at KB Corp, how everything flowed, how I woke up every morning looking forward to going to work. My productivity was high. So was everybody else's. We were all really engaged. People even said they enjoyed working with me, though the truth is I spent a lot of time alone. I could feel myself smiling at the memory. My work life then couldn't have been any more different from the nightmare I was experiencing now.

"I just had a thought," I said. "At KB I didn't have to deal with people much except to come up with innovative answers to their technological questions. Under those circumstances, it wasn't such a challenge to stay in Learner."

"I see what you mean," Joseph said. "Applying those same principles to your present leadership role might be a challenge. Humans aren't machines."

"That's what my wife keeps telling me," I said.

We both chuckled.

"So let me see if I understand you correctly," Joseph said. "With technology problems, your Learner curiosity is natural and easy. You're really good at that. You have specific questions that help you to step outside yourself to make objective observations, to test your assumptions, and assess what's going on. In those situations, you understand

that whatever you come up with is neither good nor bad—
it's simply information. Thomas Edison was famous for
telling people how it took thousands of failures to invent the
electric light bulb and that each failure contributed to that
final successful solution.

"I'm giving you new tools to take advantage of what you
already know how to do. When you can recognize Judger,
distinguish it from Learner, and switch to Learner whenever
you choose, that's self-coaching, and you're well on your
way to taking charge of your life—at work *and* at home."

Suddenly something clicked for me. I turned my attention to the Choice Map as Joseph spoke and focused on the
Switching Lane. "Switching is what makes it possible to
change," I exclaimed. "Switching is where the action is!"

> Switching is what makes it possible to
> change. Switching is where the action is!

Joseph nodded emphatically. "Yes! You've got it!" he
exclaimed. "The ability to switch literally puts you in charge
of change. Being able to nonjudgmentally observe your own
Judger and then ask a Switching question—well, that's about
the most powerful and courageous thing anybody can do for
themselves. It's the operational heart of change, what many
people call *self-management,* or *self-regulation.* Actually,

combining the willingness and the ability to switch leads not only to change, it also makes us able to sustain change, because we're observing and asking ourselves Learner questions moment by moment by moment. Switching mindsets can literally give us new eyes and new ears."

Joseph's enthusiasm was contagious.

"So those hot buttons that once might have triggered our reaction to fight or flee now signal us that we're in Judger," I said. "We're actually transforming triggers into signals. And we reach for a Switching question to reposition ourselves in Learner. We're pulling our own strings instead of giving that power away to someone else."

"Exactly," Joseph said. "Exactly!"

I was eager to learn more, especially the parts about change and sustaining change and how that could improve my results at work. But a glance at the clock told me that today's meeting was coming to an end.

CHAPTER 7

See with New Eyes, Hear with New Ears

Authentic listening is not easy. We hear the words, but rarely do we really slow down to listen and to squint with our ears, to hear the emotions, fears, and underlying concerns.

Kevin Cashman

We started our next meeting with a question that had been disturbing me since early in my conversations with Joseph. "Maybe it's just wishful thinking," I began, "but given the problems Judger throws our way . . ."

Joseph lifted his hand, signaling me to stop, and replied, "None of us can avoid slipping into Judger from time to time. It's only human." Then he smiled enigmatically and added, "But you can free yourself from Judger by simply accepting that part of yourself. *Judger is not the problem; it's how we relate to Judger that makes all the difference.* It's such a simple formula: Judger-Switch-Learner. But nobody can make it work without beginning with acceptance.

"Huh? That doesn't make sense. How can I be free of something that's part of me?"

"It does sound like a paradox, doesn't it," Joseph said. "But it *is* possible. Simple acceptance of what is creates a

level playing field so that change is really possible. But lev-
eling the field can also be challenging, especially if Judger
whispers in your ear a lot. Did Alexa ever tell you about her
husband Stan's breakthrough?"

"She mentioned it," I replied. "You helped him to make
a pile of money, as I understand it."

"He's very proud of that story," Joseph said. "He used
the QT tools to earn his way into my Hall of Fame. Stan,
as Alexa may have told you, is in the investment business.
Accepting his own Judger turned out to be very profitable
for him!

"Some years back, Stan was a very judgmental guy and
very stuck in needing to be right. He didn't think of himself that way, but many people around him did. If he had
a run-in with someone, or heard gossip about that person
that wasn't flattering, he'd just write that person off. Stan
will tell you that he clung to his assumptions and opinions
like a bull terrier to a bone. He turned down many business
opportunities on the basis of rumor, idle gossip, and guilt
by association. He justified it all as a way of minimizing
risk—which was only partially true.

"One time he made a very large investment in a promising start-up technology company. About a year later, the
company hired a CEO who'd been employed by a firm that
was implicated in a big financial scandal. Although this
new guy had been exonerated of any wrongdoing, Stan
insisted that where there was smoke there was fire. He

was on the verge of pulling his money out but was also in a great deal of conflict about the whole thing. Except for the CEO they'd hired, the company seemed to be doing everything right.

"About this time, Sarah and I had dinner with Stan and Alexa. We were discussing the Learner/Judger material, and Alexa encouraged Stan to question his assumptions and use Switching questions to evaluate his investment decision. She suggested he apply the *ABCD Choice Process* to that issue. That's the tool I've been promising to tell you about. Stan agreed to try it, and he was amazed at what a big difference it made. Here's how the ABCD Choice Process works:

ABCD Choice Process

A **Aware**

Am I in Judger? Is this working?

B **Breathe!**

Do I need to step back, pause, and gain perspective?

C **Curiosity**

What's really going on (with me, others, the situation)?

What am I missing?

D **Decide**

What's my decision? What do I choose?

A—Aware. *Am I in Judger?* Stan was very funny about this. After we described the characteristics of Judger, Stan amazingly admitted that an awful lot of what we described applied to him. His response surprised us: "Being in Judger is my forte!" We all laughed, though we knew he was beginning to look at his behavior more honestly.

B—Breathe! *Do I need to pause, step back, and look at this situation more objectively?* Stan smiled at this question, took a deep breath, paused, and shortly admitted that he was being anything but objective, especially because so much money was at stake. He really distrusted this new CEO, though he'd never even spoken with the man.

C—Curiosity. *What's happening here? What are the facts? What am I missing or avoiding?* We asked Stan if he'd done anything to collect objective information. Did he have everything he needed to make a responsible judgment? Stan realized that he'd never gotten past his distaste for what he'd heard about the guy. But facts? No, he admitted that he actually had no facts. That was a real eye opener for him.

D—Decide. *What's my decision? What's my choice?* Well, by then Stan realized that he didn't have all the information he needed to make a wise choice. And because of his large investment he owed it to himself to check things out. A month later Stan called to tell me he'd checked around and found out the new CEO was a good guy. It was his awareness and acceptance of Judger that allowed him to scrutinize his assumptions and open his mind about the new CEO. Long story short, Stan left his money in, the company went public two years later, and he made a fortune.

"The whole situation made Stan stop and think. It was a real wake-up call for him. Having realized how much money his Judger almost cost him, Stan tells me he now uses ABCD all the time. It's become an integral part of self-coaching for him. He even jokes that he's starting to hard-wire those questions into his brain! None of this would have happened if he hadn't been able to simply observe and accept the Judger part of himself instead of pushing it away. Using the ABCD process begins with awareness and acceptance, then builds on it. Stan certainly reaped the rewards!

"If you met Stan today, you'd still notice that he can be opinionated and judgmental. He knows that part of himself very well and accepts it, but now he doesn't allow it to blind him in making decisions. He even has a sense of humor about his Judger."

"Great story!" I said, and I really meant it. I found the ABCD formula in my workbook and jotted down a few notes.

"Think about Stan making all that money and my wife finally being successful with her weight," Joseph noted. "If they had continued wasting time being judgmental about their own Judger, they wouldn't have even gotten to first base in making the changes they wanted."

"This all sounds great. It really does. But here's something I'm stuck on. Learner can sound soft. Leaders have to be strong and decisive. Leaders have to act tough and make the tough calls. I don't see how being more of a Learner can help me do that."

"How about Alexa," Joseph countered. "How does she handle the tough calls?"

"Point made," I responded quickly, thinking back to some difficult decisions she had made that I wouldn't have wanted to face myself. She could be hard as nails when the situation demanded it, yet everyone who worked for her still felt respected even when she challenged us.

Joseph continued, "There's an important difference between 'Learner tough' and 'Judger tough.' You can get the job done from either position. However, a Learner leader displays the kind of toughness that builds loyalty and respect as well as cooperation and risk-taking. Judger leaders are more likely to generate fear, mistrust, and conflict in the people around them."

Was Joseph referring to my leadership style and nightmare team? Rather than bringing that up, I challenged him about another reservation I had about Learner.

"Doesn't Learner slow things down?" I blurted out. "Work is just one pressure and deadline after another. Sometimes I'm staggered by the amount of things I need to get done and how fast they have to happen. If I had to be in Learner all the time, wouldn't it take forever to get things done? I mean, wouldn't I end up more behind than ever?"

Joseph answered my question with more of his own. "How many times, when you were in a rush, have you made a mistake, blamed yourself or others, and then had to do it all over? How much extra time did *that* take? In your haste, how many times have you been impatient or impolite to someone and then noticed that he or she didn't talk to you much after that? What's the cost in time, results, and even loyalty when you treat people like that?"

I just stared at him. It felt like he had been watching me in my office all day long, five days a week. Then he added, "That's what happens when Judger takes over at work. On the other hand, I've heard over and over, from the folks in my Question Thinking Hall of Fame, that Learner actually helps them save time and increase productivity. In fact, one of them commented that speed and efficiency are not at all the same thing. Then he joked that Judger puts speed bumps on efficiency as well as effectiveness!

Judger puts speed bumps on efficiency as well as effectiveness!

"Judger makes speed bumps. I like that," I said. "It sure seems like life would be a lot simpler if we could all just rec-ognize and accept Judger in ourselves, switch to Learner, and operate from there."

"How true!" Joseph said. "That's one of the ultimate

goals of Question Thinking. Imagine what work would be like if people did this most of the time. You would have a Learner culture; you could even say you have a Learner organization. And what about your team, Ben? The one you complain about so much. Are they in Judger or Learner most of the time? You know that teams and even organizations follow the mood and behavior of their leaders. As the leader of the team, *your* results will only get better if *theirs* do." He paused for a moment, then added: "Think of what we've been discussing as a *practice*, in the way that some people practice yoga, or mindfulness, or meditation. It's something you give quality attention to daily, sometimes hour by hour, sometimes moment by moment. You get better at it the more you practice. As one of my clients put it, this practice rewired his brain. I think it's true. Soon you'll see with new eyes and hear with new ears."

Joseph glanced at his watch. "We've been talking quite a while. We can take a short break and then go onto the next step, or wait until the next time we get together. What do you want to do?"

I was torn. I needed time to digest what we'd covered so far. But frankly, I was eager to hear the rest of what Joseph would tell me. I knew it would help with conversations that would soon be coming up with Charles — and also with Grace. It took only a second to make my decision. "Okay, let's go for it!"

CHAPTER 8

Learner Teams and Judger Teams

It's not differences that divide us. It's our judgments about each other that do.

Margaret J. Wheatley

During our break, I started remembering what it had been like to work at KB. It had been very different from what I was now experiencing at QTec. When I compared the two experiences—KB versus QTec—there wasn't a doubt in my mind that at KB I had mostly been in Learner. As a research engineer and head tech guy, I did most of my work alone, then reported my findings to the team, taking their questions and providing answers. It was easy to be in Learner most of the time. By contrast, at QTec it was apparent that I was in Judger more often than I cared to admit. No matter where I looked, especially with my team, something seemed to be going wrong or somebody was failing to do what they were supposed to. How could I avoid going into Judger? As Joseph and I continued our meeting that day, I hesitantly shared this observation with him and said, "I'm not sure where to take it from here."

"I think I can best respond to that with a folk tale," Joseph replied. "You've probably heard of the mythologist Joseph Campbell. He was famous for coming up with exactly the right story for every situation. Here's one I heard many years ago.

"It seems a farmer was out working his field when his plow caught on something, and it wouldn't budge. The horse reared up and the farmer cursed. After calming the horse the farmer yanked back on the braces. But the plow still wouldn't budge. Because he was an impatient man his first reaction was to go into Judger. Had a rock or other obstacle broken his plowshare? That could mean losing at least two days' work while he hauled the broken parts to the blacksmith! Cursing, he began digging around to free the plow. To his surprise, he discovered that it was caught on an iron ring buried six inches under the ground.

"After freeing his plow, the farmer got curious. He cleared away some of the dirt and pulled on the iron ring. Off came the lid of an ancient chest. He peeked down inside it. Before him, glittering in the sun, lay a treasure of precious jewels and gold.

"This story reminds us that it is often by confronting our toughest obstacles that we find our greatest strengths and possibilities, but sometimes we've got to dig deep to find them. Campbell had a phrase for it: *Where you stumble, there your treasure is.* To uncover that treasure you'd ask yourself questions like: *What could I discover? What haven't I noticed before? What might be valuable here?*"

> "Where you stumble, there your treasure is."
>
> *Joseph Campbell*

"That might be fine and well. But I'm still not seeing how all this is going to help *me*. Where's the treasure in this mess of mine?"

Joseph easily took up my challenge. "How about doing a little excavating," he said. "To start with, let's look at how your mindsets and your questions affect people around you." He leaned back in his chair and took a deep breath." - For example, what about that team you're heading up? How often are you in Judger when you meet with them?"

"Truthfully? Just about every meeting lately!"

"And how would you say you communicate with the members of your team?"

"Communicate? That's a laugh! Listen, I told you how awful our meetings are. When I do call a meeting nobody has much to offer. They sit on their hands and wait for me to tell them what to do. Finally I talk, and Charles barrages me with his interminable questions. Doesn't matter what I say, he questions everything."

"Think of yourself as the farmer in Campbell's story," Joseph continued. "When you're with your team, are you cursing the fact that your plow got stuck, or are you getting curious about finding the door to the treasure? Are you looking for who's to blame or are you looking for what's working and what might be possible? Are you asking yourself questions like: *How can I show them I have the right answer?* Or are you asking: *What can we discover and accomplish together? What could they contribute that I haven't thought of yet?*"

I wasn't sure what I did, but I knew it wasn't what Joseph was suggesting. "I guess you'll have to clue me in here."

"Okay. You've been in conferences with Alexa. How does she conduct her meetings? What does she say and do? How do her meetings affect you?"

"I look forward to Alexa's meetings," I told Joseph. "They're always enlivening. I come away with new ideas to pursue. I feel like charging back to my office to start acting on them. But I've never been able to figure out what she does to generate that kind of energy and excitement."

The moment those words were out of my mouth, it hit me. "Alexa asks questions," I said. "Her meetings are all about questions. But not interrogating kinds of questions. She really piques everyone's curiosity. Her questions are Learner ones and they motivate us, sometimes even inspire us."

Joseph sat back in his chair a moment before leaning forward enthusiastically. "Alexa's questions motivate you to contribute your best. She inspires people to abandon Judger and operate from Learner. She likes to say that 'Learner begets Learner. And Judger begets Judger.' You could even call Alexa a Learner leader." Joseph paused for a moment and then asked, "How do you think her questions are different from yours?"

Learner begets Learner.

And Judger begets Judger.

"Alexa has her style, I have mine," I said, getting a little defensive.

"Do you ask questions?"

"Sure I ask questions. Besides talking to my people in person, I send out emails and texts asking what they've accomplished. Or what they haven't accomplished, which is more to the point lately. I get very few replies, which is pretty maddening."

"When they do answer, how do you listen? How do you respond?"

"It depends. If the answer is any good, I might jot it down. But lately, I leave those meetings with nothing."

"Describe what the experience of listening is like for you," Joseph said.

That wasn't difficult. "Mostly I've been pretty annoyed and impatient," I replied, "especially when a person's answer doesn't come close to solving the problem, or when it shows that person is not following my plan. I get the impression nobody really cares."

"In situations like those, what's your attitude toward your colleagues? Are you in Learner or Judger most of the time?"

"What else! Judger, of course. But nobody is contributing a darn thing . . . if they would only . . ."

Joseph held up his hand. "Whoa! Hold on, my friend. When you're with your team, it sounds like you're listening with Judger ears and thinking with Judger questions like: *Are they going to screw up again?* and *How are they going to disappoint me this time?*"

"Sure, those sound like my questions. What else would I be asking . . ." I suddenly stopped. "Boy, I just stubbed my toe on the iron ring in the story you told me, didn't I?"

"You sure did. Good observation! And like the farmer, your first reaction was to go Judger—which is natural enough," Joseph said. "Now do what the farmer did next. Get curious. Ask yourself, 'What's happening here?' Think about your team, and this time follow the Learner path."

"Follow the Learner path with my team? You've got to be kidding," I said. "Besides, how would I do that?"

"For starters, listen to them with Learner ears. Reset yourself in Learner mindset before you meet with your team. Try the kinds of questions Alexa asks, like: *What do I appreciate about them? What are the best strengths of each one? How can I help them collaborate most productively? How can we stay on the Learner path together?*

"I'll bet you can see how those Learner questions would change everything in a meeting. Alexa's questions create a Learner environment. They invite everyone—including you—to listen more respectfully, with patience and care. With Learner questions we listen in order to understand the other person rather than to find out who's right or wrong. That makes it possible for everyone to get curious, feel safe taking risks, and participate fully, even when they're facing tough challenges."

"It's the tough challenges part that gets me in trouble," I argued. "We've got some big problems and nobody is willing to speak up, much less take them on. Plus, there are so many major decisions we disagree on. We just can't seem to get through the conflicts to the other side. That's when I get frustrated and start feeling like nothing is ever going to work out. I think myself right down into the Judger Pit."

"Even though you'll never be pure Learner or a saint, including with your team, you can learn to choose where you put your attention moment to moment. Any attention you give to Judger isn't available to give to Learner. Accept Judger, practice Learner. Imprint those words on your brain. It's as important for teams as it is for individuals."

Accept Judger, practice Learner.
It's as important for teams as it is
for individuals!

"So that's why Alexa's meetings are so great," I reflected. "They're Learner environments, as you say. I always have the sense that we have her full attention and that she really cares about what we have to say. If she ever goes Judger, I'm sure it's just for a fleeting visit." I had a sudden insight. *"All she asks are Learner questions, and lots of them.* Plus, I'll bet she gets an almost perfect score on asking questions and listening deeply and generously with just about everyone she knows. That's why she's called the *inquiring leader,* isn't it?"

"That's it," Joseph said. "Alexa genuinely cares about what people have to say. Not only does she ask Learner questions, she also listens with Learner ears. Alexa's listening is focused by questions such as: *What's valuable here? What's to be learned from that comment? How can this contribute to what we're working on?* The questions she listens with help her teams turn into Learner teams very quickly. She expects to find the treasure, she looks for it, and because of that she often finds it.

"The Choice Map can help you do this with your team, too. Look at it again. So far, we've been thinking about it as a guide for how an *individual* thinks, behaves, and relates. Now, let's consider it as a guide for *teams.* Start thinking in terms of Learner teams and Judger teams.

"I think of Learner teams as being typically high performing and Judger teams as being typically low performing. When researchers explored what distinguished high-performing teams from low-performing ones, can you guess what they found?"

Part of me didn't even want to know; another part was intrigued. But I decided not to guess. "No, what?" I replied.

"First of all, the high-performing teams had more positive emotions than the low-performing ones. That's not a big surprise. But what I found revealing was that the low-performing teams were low on *inquiry*—that is, on asking questions—and high on *advocacy*—that is, on pushing a particular viewpoint rather than listening to anybody else."

"So the bottom line," I said, "is if you want high performance, focus on Learner."

"Yes," Joseph said. "But there's more. The research also showed that high-performing teams consistently had a good balance between inquiry and advocacy—that has to have been *Learner* inquiry and *Learner* advocacy. It means that people feel free to ask tough questions and have genuine open debate. They can even argue and have conflicts, yet the atmosphere remains essentially Learner."

"That's exactly what happens with Alexa's meetings," I said. "This is great!"

"It's what Alexa calls a Learner Alliance," Joseph said. "It's when team members work together to stay on the Learner path. That's completely opposite of what happens when members of a team go Judger and end up in what I call a *Judger stand-off*. That's when each person just defends his own opinion and believes he's the only one who is right.

He turns a deaf ear to anyone else's ideas. It's like everyone is in *Judger jail* together. Nothing gets done, and everyone blames someone else. That's the real cost of Judger when it takes over a team like that."

It's a Learner Alliance when team members work together to stay on the Learner path.

When I pictured the Choice Map I could clearly imagine Alexa's whole team jogging happily along the Learner path, having set off on their journey with Learner questions. Their attention was free to focus on new solutions and possibilities. Alexa's team would certainly qualify as a high-performing one. And my team? Most of my people were down at the bottom of the map, mired in the mud of the Judger Pit—and I'd put them there! I hated to admit that most of the time I was being a Judger leader. But accepting that fact was the only way I'd ever get them out.

"I'm just the opposite of Alexa," I mumbled. "She seems to create a balanced Learner environment almost automatically."

"She wasn't always that way. Like most of us," Joseph noted, "she was automatically more Judger to start with. It usually takes effort and intention to turn the tide and become more naturally Learner. Think about it as deliberately training your brain to do things it doesn't automatically know how to do. Like anything—learning to drive a car or operate a computer or learning to ride a bike—it requires close attention at first but soon becomes second nature."

"This is a lot to take in," I said. "When I first walked into your office, truthfully I was just looking for a quick fix. What you're offering is obviously a lot bigger."

Joseph nodded.

"Can't you narrow it down to a few words of advice?" I joked.

"How often do people really take advice?"

He was right, of course. "I guess I'm an expert at not taking advice."

"Aren't we all?" Joseph replied. "Even though it's hard to resist, I try to avoid giving advice. I know that if I ask good questions, people are smart enough to come up with their own best answers. Our own advice is the only kind most of us listen to and act on anyway . . . But I do have a suggestion for you, Ben." Joseph flashed his signature mischievous grin. "Do you want to hear it?"

"Sure," I said—and we both laughed.

"Alexa is a great model for what you and I are working on. She went through a lot of things similar to what you've been through in order to accomplish what she has. Next time you meet with Alexa, ask her to tell you about her experiences. I'm sure she'd be happy to."

Good suggestion! I thought. Then I asked Joseph if there were any other things I should bring up with Alexa.

Joseph nodded. "There is something else. Alexa came up with this terrific Question Thinking practice she calls Q-Storming®. It's sort of like brainstorming except that you're looking for new questions instead of answers and ideas. Ask her to explain Q-Storming to you. There's also a tool about it in your workbook. Alexa credits it with being the catalyst for many of her most important breakthroughs."

Now that sounded really intriguing—and promising. That's where Joseph and I ended our conversation that day.

Down on the street a few minutes later, I cut through the park across from the Pearl Building into an open playing field where an older boy was helping a younger one learn to ride his bicycle. I stopped to watch.

In spite of spills and near falls, they were having fun. There were shouts of encouragement, along with cries of despair as the younger boy made yet another mistake and tumbled to the ground. Each time the younger boy fell, the older one rushed to his side to give assistance and support to try again.

Finally, the younger boy caught on. He rode off, covering 50 feet or so, with the older boy chasing after him, whooping and hollering cries of victory. I caught myself thinking *Why are adults so damned competitive? Why are they so uncooperative, always looking for ways to show up the other guy? Why did I have to put up with people like Charles?* I was getting angry.

I turned around to catch one last glimpse of the kids

before climbing into my car. Now the two of them were standing beside the upright bike, laughing together. The expressions on their faces told me everything. The new bike rider glowed with the excitement of having achieved something new. And this experience had triggered that universal *I-did-that* response that I must admit always gives me a glow. I reached for the ignition key and thought: *Wouldn't it be amazing if our team could work together just like those kids? I wonder what it would take to make that happen—to trigger that I-did-that response again and again.*

At that moment I realized I'd done something that was still quite new for me. I had transformed Judger questions into Learner ones. *Not bad*, I thought. A chill of excitement ran up the whole length of my spine. I guess those kids weren't the only ones who could experience the pleasure of the *I-did-that* response. I couldn't wait to share this with Joseph. That's when it occurred to me that maybe I really could follow Alexa's example—turn my team into a Learner team by becoming a Learner leader. The inquiring coach, as Alexa called Joseph, was really onto something! I wanted to find out what else Joseph had up his sleeve. I was beginning to feel real hope that maybe it wasn't too late to salvage my career.

CHAPTER 9

When the Magic Works

When you enter a mindset, you enter a new world.

Carol S. Dweck

Over breakfast a few days later, Grace told me about what had happened with Jennifer, the young woman she'd been having so much trouble with at work. Grace even apologized for calling me during the day just to vent.

"I kept the Choice Map on my desk all day," Grace said. "Two Learner questions kept jumping out at me — *What do I want for myself, for others, and for the situation?* And *What are my choices?* When I applied those questions to Jennifer, I realized I wanted her to start showing more common sense and initiative. So, I tried some new questions. I asked myself *Why does Jennifer need so much direction from me?* I became truly curious after I realized I didn't know. Was she afraid of acting on her own? Or worried that I'd fire her for making a mistake? I also wondered whether she had more going for her than I'd given her credit for. The next time she came to me for help I asked her a question instead of just giving her instructions. I inquired with real curiosity, 'How would you solve this problem if you were the boss?'

"That single question opened up a very productive conversation. Jennifer confessed that she was, indeed, afraid of me. She thought if she didn't do exactly what I expected her to, I'd fire her. This is what had happened with her previous boss, and she didn't want it to ever happen again. That talk changed everything. She told me that afterward she felt more comfortable about taking initiative and working on her own. She also came up with some good ideas for solving her own problem. She was obviously very pleased with herself. I congratulated her—and told her how happy I was that we had opened up communication between us.

"I'm really surprised, and glad. And, you know what? Asking Learner questions made me feel a lot better at the end of the day. I realize now I was being unfair to Jennifer. I had been assuming she was asking all those questions because she was incompetent. She really isn't. It's just that she believed she had to check everything out with me before acting on her own. That crowded out any room for her to be creative or take any initiative."

As Grace told me the story of her breakthrough with Jennifer, I was relieved she didn't ask me about any results I'd gotten from working with Joseph's ideas. It's true I'd had some shifts in my thinking and was somewhat hopeful rather than just resigned. But I didn't have much to show for my efforts yet. And my team was still a nightmare.

When I finally left home I was at least 20 minutes late. Traffic was piling up on the freeway. A mile past my on-ramp, the highway had practically turned into a parking lot. Cars were creeping along for as far as I could see, and in all four lanes. I was getting frantic. I didn't even notice my Judger mindset had kicked in. At least not right away.

Then traffic stopped completely. I gritted my teeth, set the car in park, and pulled out my phone to check for messages. My secretary had texted several reminders, which did nothing to lessen my stress. I was already anxious about that morning's meeting with Alexa and was dreading the one with Charles this afternoon. I wasn't ready for either, least of all the latter.

I slapped the steering wheel in frustration, muttering something about how one guy, stupid enough to run out of gas, had ruined the whole day for half the city. *Who was the idiot responsible? I didn't need this! Was it so difficult to keep your tank filled? Didn't that fool realize . . .*

I felt like my head would explode if traffic didn't start moving. Tension spread through my whole body, like an electric sensation shooting out to every muscle. These sensations were all too familiar. Mostly I was aware of the muscles in my legs and back tensing up as if getting ready to fight or run, or maybe both, if that's possible. But here I was frozen to the spot, in traffic that gave no signs of moving . . . and I *had* to get to the office.

I suddenly stopped myself. *Ben, you're solidly in Judger*, I said, my voice muffled by the sounds of the idling engine. And then I actually laughed at myself. My observer self to rescue! Could Judger really cause all these grossly unpleasant physical symptoms? Could it be Judger feeding my frustration and these angry thoughts? This upset wasn't only in my head. That's for sure. It may have started as my own thoughts or feelings, but there wasn't a grain of doubt that Judger affected every part of my body. I could almost feel it in my brain, clouding my thinking.

About then I heard sirens and a few minutes later an ambulance sped past in the emergency lane. Accident! I switched on the radio for the traffic report. Two people badly hurt. Oh, man! I felt pretty embarrassed about jumping to the conclusion that some jerk had run out of gas. Who was the *real* jerk—me! My attention then shifted to the people who were hurt. I hoped they were going to be okay. What was wrong with me, getting so worked up over a story I'd made up in my own mind? I noticed that my stress softened a little as my thoughts focused on the victims of the crash: *Will they get help soon enough? Are they in pain? How will this accident affect their lives?*

Ten minutes later traffic still wasn't moving, and I have to admit I started to get frustrated and stressed again. Worries about my meeting with Charles intruded. My thoughts churned around in my brain, fueling my long-standing annoyance with him. I sure needed help with this one! What would Joseph tell me? I heard his voice in my head, reminding me how important it is to change my questions, especially about Charles and my team.

Yesterday Joseph told me to find a real situation to test out what I'd been learning about recovering from a Judger hijack. The meeting with Charles this afternoon was about as real as it gets. But what questions would help me get out of what Grace called my *Judger head?* What Learner questions could help me with Charles? Traffic suddenly moved forward a hundred yards or so before it stopped again. In those few moments I realized I had already stepped onto the Switching Lane with the questions I'd just asked myself.

Joseph kept suggesting that whenever I was able to catch myself in Judger I should stop and congratulate myself for becoming more aware. Then I should step back and find out what I was asking myself. At that moment the question that popped into my mind was *how can I get out of here?* Obviously, there wasn't much choice about that. I was stuck until traffic started moving. Then something else Joseph said came back to me: "We don't have much control over what happens, but we can choose how we relate to what happens." Almost immediately, a new question came to mind: *What can I do to right now to make the best use of this time?*

We don't have much control over what happens, but we can choose how we relate to what happens.

It took only a second to come up with an answer to that one. I grabbed my phone off the seat beside me and scrolled to Joseph's number. He answered immediately.

"Ben here," I said. "Do you have a minute? I'm stuck in traffic and going a little nuts."

Joseph was silent for a moment, then laughed: "Did you try saying *beam me up, Scotty?*"

"How'd you know I was a Trekkie?" I laughed and almost instantly my mood lightened.

"I've got a meeting with Charles this afternoon," I explained. "I realize I have to get into Learner mindset to even have a chance of it going well. I'm worried that I'll blow it. Where do I begin?"

"Good question," Joseph said. "Can you write something down?"

"Sure," I said. "Go ahead."

As I sat there in stalled traffic, Joseph dictated three questions which I recorded on my smartphone: *What assumptions am I making? How else can I think about this?* And *What is the other person thinking, feeling, and wanting?*" Joseph explained that these questions were from his *Top 12 Questions for Success*, one of the tools I'd find in the QT Workbook.

I looked at the first question: *What assumptions am I making?* That was easy enough. Where Charles was concerned my assumptions were unavoidable. I'd beaten him out of a big promotion. Guys in that position can be dangerous. I'd be a fool to drop my guard with him. I was sure

Ben's Three Questions

What assumptions am I making?

How else can I think about this?

What is the other person thinking, feeling,
  and wanting?

nothing would make Charles happier than to see me fail. I
was also sure he'd do whatever he could to make that happen. Then he could step into my position and have what he
wanted. Who wouldn't assume you had to watch your back
with guys like that?

Sure, these were just assumptions. I wasn't denying that. But there are situations where going with your
assumptions is the safest route, and this was one of them.
So far, the problems I was having with Charles seemed real
enough to me.As I thought about all this, something I'd
read in the Learner/Judger Mindset Chart kept nagging at
me: *Was I defending my assumptions instead of questioning them?* Though still unsettled, I turned to Joseph's second question: *How else can I think about this?* Something
Grace had said clicked in my mind—how her assumptions
about Jennifer had damaged their relationship. Grace had
used the Choice Map to find a different way of relating to
Jennifer. Could I do the same with Charles?

I began to wonder about other possibilities. For

example, what would happen if I reconsidered some of my opinions about Charles? What if his questions weren't aimed at making me look bad, as I'd assumed? What if he just wanted to make sure we'd covered all our bases? Then I remembered Joseph telling me about winning teams and their balance between inquiry and advocacy. What if Charles's endless questions were just his way to encourage more thoughtful discussions? I was pretty sure I was giving Charles more credit than he was due—but maybe not. The more I considered other ways of thinking about the situation, the less certain I was about my old opinions.

I decided to try something new in my meeting with Charles that afternoon. When he walked in, I would suspend thinking that he was after my job and out to sabotage me. Instead, I would try to be neutral, to adopt a mindset of *not-knowing,* as Joseph had suggested, rather than thinking I had to have all the answers. The moment this thought crossed my mind, new ideas tumbled into place. Even though I wasn't ready to totally trust Joseph's theories, for the first time I was willing to give Charles the benefit of the doubt. This was great. I actually had something that was new, that was innovative and that I could *do.*

I was just starting to consider Joseph's third question—*What is the other person thinking, feeling, and wanting?*—when traffic began to inch forward. I put that question on hold. But even as I got under way, new possibilities began unfolding in my mind. If Charles was merely being inquisitive, what was he wanting or needing from me? I remembered a conversation we'd had my first day on the job. He'd said, "I have to tell you, I'm disappointed I didn't get the promotion. This is a great company and my family likes this town. I don't want to have to move them. I'll do everything I can to make this company successful."

His comment that he'd do anything to make this company successful still bothered me. What exactly did he mean by that? My assumption had been that this included going after my job. Could I have misread Charles's intentions? Could there be another way of interpreting what he'd said?

I arrived at my office way behind schedule. With less than 10 minutes before my meeting with Alexa, I sat down at my computer, typed in her name and that of the magazine I'd seen in Joseph's Hall of Fame gallery. The article about her popped up instantly.

Fast Company Magazine had chosen Alexa for their Woman of the Year award before we met at KB. I scanned the story. It told about her stepping into the CEO position at KB right after it went into Chapter 11. She had been brought in to turn the company around. Everyone had advised her against it. If she didn't succeed, it could destroy her career. She took the risk and accomplished the impossible, and three years later she took the company global.

I skipped ahead several paragraphs. Alexa was quoted as saying she owed her success to "simply changing the kinds of questions I was asking." In the next paragraph she named her personal coach and mentor: Joseph S. Edwards. Who else?

Moments after reading the article, I was seated in Alexa's office. Although my intention was to ask about her experiences with Joseph and about Q-Storming, my curiosity got the best of me and I found myself asking about the *Fast Company* article. "You never told me about your getting the *Woman of the Year* award," I said. "I just read about it on the Internet."

"Oh, yes. They labeled me *The Inquiring Leader*. You know what? I don't think my interviewer had ever heard of a CEO making a point of asking lots of questions. It was a great novelty to him!" She chuckled at the thought. "It seems like such a simple thing. Most leaders do more telling than asking. That's why they never find out what's really going on. All too often they base their decisions about strategic direction, and even about their own people, on insufficient or inaccurate information."

"They make assumptions instead," I added, "which they never test."

"Exactly. Well, that just didn't make any sense to me."

I heard Joseph's teachings in her words, but what she said was obviously authentic for her.

"Joseph and I have been discussing Learner and Judger mindsets and the Choice Map," I said. "He told me I'm not the only person in this room who ever ran into problems with Judger." I checked her expression to make sure she didn't mind my saying that. She was smiling, so I continued. "He suggested you might share a few of your own Judger challenges with your old company. What were some of the Judger questions you started out with?"

"You know, in retrospect it seems so simple I almost laugh. The kinds of questions I'd been asking were along the order of *who's to blame for the mess we're in?* I was lying awake nights trying to figure out whom I should fire—and worrying that it might be me! Then, one day, working with Joseph, I started coming up with new questions. I think the first one was *how can we avoid making so many mistakes?* Joseph thought that was a good beginning but suggested I could come up with something even better."

"You mean a stronger Learner question?"

"Exactly," Alexa said. "The one I figured out was *How can we build on our strengths and successes?* I really took that question seriously and started asking it all the time. I got everyone on track with that new question. I could see that the Judger questions I'd been asking made everything more difficult. We had had what I'd call a high Judger culture. Judger drained our energy, pretty much killed our enthusiasm, divided us so we were always looking for someone to blame—in short, Judger derailed us and had us going in all directions at once, none of which were very productive. That new Learner question piqued our curiosity and invited us to take positive, focused, and creative actions together. Joseph said to use the new question to build a Learner culture, and that's what I set out to do. Pretty soon we were turning things around in remarkable ways. Until then, I'd never really grasped the truth about the power of questions, that they can lead us to failure or to success. It was a big shift for me, and for all of us."

"What was it about that new question that made such a difference?" I asked.

"Maybe an example Joseph gave us would make this clearer. It had to do with a study that was done with two comparable basketball teams. Team A was coached with an emphasis on preventing mistakes on the court. Day after day, they reviewed videos that focused on their errors. Those mistakes got grooved in their brains. By contrast, Team B was coached with an emphasis on building on their successes. Day after day, they reviewed videos that focused on their most successful plays. So Team B's successes got grooved in their brains.

"To put it simply, Team A focused on what was wrong. Team B focused on what was right. I'm sure you can guess which team had the greatest improvement by the end of the season."

"The one that built on their successes, of course."

"That's absolutely right," Alexa said. "In fact, by the end the difference in these teams' performances was startling. As I recall, Team A actually had a slight reduction in their accomplishments. Team B improved by nearly 30 percent. That's all it took to convince me of the power of

asking the right kinds of questions. I applied those same principles to our floundering company, and that's when dramatic changes began to occur. Not only did our productivity increase, but coming to work was more enjoyable, even fun. Creativity and morale were boosted. There was higher energy throughout the company. The whole place began operating on Learner principles and shifting to Learner questions—the way that Learner begets Learner—and it all happened in months instead of years. I guess you just read the rest of the story."

Alexa paused as she recalled that time of her life. "What could be more natural or obvious," she continued, "than to *simply ask*? How else can you get a complete picture of what's going on? How else can you get people contributing so enthusiastically? What else would make people feel respected—and that what they said and did really *mattered*? Could we ever discover or learn or create anything new without being curious first? Curiosity is one of our greatest assets. I'm sure Joseph has emphasized this to you. Curiosity is the fast track to Learner. It's high-test fuel for progress and change!"

> Curiosity is the fast track to Learner.

As Alexa talked, I was thinking about how important it was to check my assumptions about Charles. *Were my*

*Judger questions blinding me from seeing something impor-
tant about him? Did I really know why Charles asked so many
questions?* Before I had a chance to stop myself the words
popped out of my mouth.

"He's just asking me all those questions because he's
curious. He wants to understand!"

Alexa looked at me with concern. "What in heaven's
name are you talking about?"

"Sorry, Alexa, I was just thinking out loud," I replied.
"This conversation has really gotten me all fired up about
my team and our project."-

"It sure seems that you're onto something," Alexa said,
nodding her head. "And I think I can say with confidence that
your new questions are going to produce some real progress."

My mind ran back to the conversation Grace and I had
had earlier that morning. In working out her situation with
Jennifer, Grace had started by asking herself: *What do I want?*
and *What are my choices?* and then she asked: *How can I
understand her better?* I realized this last question wasn't one
I ever asked myself about people I worked with. Instantly,
other questions popped into my mind: *How does anyone ever
understand anyone else?* Joseph claimed you have to start by
getting curious about them. And then you ask them questions, Learner questions, of course. This is exactly what Grace
had done with Jennifer. What did I really understand about
Charles? I began to feel my curiosity growing and realized
new questions about him were naturally coming to mind.

I remembered that old question I'd reported to Joseph so proudly: *How can I prove I'm right?* Now I realized how that question had contributed to the team's perception of me as a know-it-all. Instead of asking *how can I prove I'm right*, I asked *how can I better understand Charles*, and *how can I better understand my team?* I was already beginning to see Charles and the team in a whole new light. What a contrast there was not only between those two questions but also in my mood and in how I was thinking about Charles!

Suddenly I remembered about Q-Storming. "Before I forget," I said. "Joseph suggested I ask you about Q-Storming. He said it was responsible for some of the best breakthroughs in your career."

Alexa's eyebrows went up. She sat forward and smiled. "It's one of my favorite subjects," she said. "You've heard of brainstorming, I'm sure. Q-Storming is like that, except you're looking for new *questions*, not for answers. It's a great way to get everyone on the same page, thinking collaboratively and out of the box. I've used it to get new thinking for all kinds of reasons: for decision making, problem solving, innovation, and even conflict resolution. I've mostly used it with groups and teams but I've also discovered how helpful it can be in one-on-one conversations."

At that moment, the phone rang on Alexa's desk. "I may have to take this," she said. "I told my secretary not to interrupt us unless a certain call came in." She reached across the desk, picked up the phone, pressed it to her ear, and exchanged a few words with her assistant. Then she shrugged apologetically and covered the receiver as she told me it was indeed the call she'd been waiting for.

On the way back to my office, I was disappointed that I hadn't learned more about Q-Storming, but I was still eager to do so. Alexa seemed like living proof that there really was some magic in Joseph's theories. Was a little of it starting to rub off on me, too? That day still held some surprises, and the person who would coach me through Q-Storming was to be the biggest surprise of all.

CHAPTER 10

Q-Storming to the Rescue

Collaboration is vital to sustain what
we call profound or really deep change,
because without it, organizations are just
overwhelmed by the forces of the status quo.

Peter Senge

With less than half an hour to get ready for my appointment with Charles, I went into self-coaching mode and
focused on the three questions Joseph had given me that
morning: *What assumptions am I making? How else might
I think about this?* And, *What is the other person thinking,
feeling, and wanting?"*

Then my secretary buzzed, announcing Charles's
arrival. In the past, I would have kept him waiting. Today,
I immediately got up and met him at the door. We shook
hands, and I asked him how he was doing. He replied that
he was fine, but he looked a little nervous. At least I wasn't
the only one! When I originally made the appointment with
him, I'd been all set for a showdown. But that was before my
meetings with Joseph. Since then, my perspective on the
problems between us had changed considerably. I offered
him a comfortable chair and asked if he'd like coffee or

anything to drink. That must have surprised him, because I'd never done that in the past. He thanked me but said he was fine, holding up a small bottle of water he'd brought along.

Yesterday while thinking about this meeting, I reviewed many of the things I'd learned from Joseph. I also considered details about how both Joseph and Alexa conducted their meetings with me. They had both asked lots of questions, but they also had a certain way of speaking that put me at ease. I always felt like they were on my side, like they wanted me to succeed. When I thought about it, I realized that both of them made our meetings a Learner experience.

I'd recalled, for example, that Joseph made sure there wasn't a desk or other physical barrier between us. This gesture made me feel that he was truly interested in what I had to say. So I was trying the same thing with Charles. With so much at stake, I wanted to do everything I could to make our meeting successful. I slid my chair from behind my desk and placed it so Charles and I were facing each other just a few feet apart near the window. Without the desk between us, establishing my authority, I felt a bit vulnerable. At first, Charles seemed a bit uncomfortable, too.

"I'm very worried about how our team is doing," I began. "In fact, we're really in trouble. So I'd like to talk some things through with you. And if it's okay, can we start with a few questions?"

Charles nodded and his eyes darted off to the right.

"Let me be quite candid with you," I continued, trying to think how Joseph would say this. "I've realized that I may have contributed to some of the problems we've been having with our team. I want to change that, and I believe the place to start is with you and me."

I paused, checking out Charles's reaction. As far as I could tell, he was attentive and engaged, though he didn't look very relaxed. When I put myself in his place, it was easy to imagine what might be going through his mind. I continued, "I've made certain judgments about you that I now believe were wrong interpretations. For example, I knew you'd been at QTec for several years and that you were in line for the job that was given to me. I'm pretty sure my arrival wasn't exactly good news for you, and I assumed you'd have trouble working under me. Am I right about this?"

Charles nodded. "I've got to confess that has been difficult. Alexa broke it to me gently enough, and made a nice salary adjustment, but that only goes so far."

His response surprised me. Had he already recognized the problem . . . and had he actually been working on it? It appeared so. For a moment I got defensive and guarded, thinking that if this were so maybe he should have gotten the job instead of me.

"Had the situation been reversed, I'd have been pretty bent out of shape myself," I said.

"I'm still working it out," Charles admitted. Let me ask you this." He paused. "How am I doing?"

"Considering that I put an awful lot off on you that really didn't belong on your shoulders, I think you're doing great."

"I'm not sure I understand," Charles said.

It wasn't easy saying what I what I said then. "I made a few assumptions about you, Charles. First, I assumed that because I was brought in over you that you'd resent me and wouldn't be able to work with me. I realize I was judging you unfairly. My second assumption had to do with all those questions you ask in our meetings."

"My questions?" Charles looked totally confused. A second or two later he had gathered his thoughts enough to say, "I don't get it. Why would my questions be a problem? You're the new guy. I need to find out what you want, where you're going to take us. How would I find out what I don't know if I don't ask?"

How would I find out what I don't know
if I don't ask?

I wasn't ready to admit to him that I'd thought his questions were aimed at showing others on the team that I didn't have all the answers. However, I told him that my job at QTec required a huge shift in the way I was accustomed to operating. "At my old company," I explained, "people came to me for answers. I was so good at it that I earned a sterling reputation as the answer man. Here at QTec I'm heading up a team and I need other people to help me find answers and implement them. Being the answer man isn't enough."

Charles took a sip of water from his bottle, then said, "A few weeks before you came aboard, Alexa brought in this guy for a training session. It was about just this sort of thing, about questions and answers. He talked about the significance of the power of questions, how they can help us to become more innovative and change our thinking, our relationships, and even an entire organization. He asked us how anyone could expect to get the best answers without first asking the best questions. One thing he said stands out in my memory. It was: *Great results begin with great questions.*"

I remembered Alexa telling me about that training session the day she hired me. She explained how she was having Joseph come in to facilitate a core training on Question Thinking. She'd invited me to attend, but I'd had scheduling conflicts with my old employer and couldn't make it. Besides, I was the answer man! Questions were the last thing on my mind back then. On top of that I barely knew what I was going to do as the leader of my team. I couldn't help but wonder how things might have been turned out had I attended Joseph's training that day. There was no doubt in my mind that Charles was describing that training, so it seemed safe to assume he also had some familiarity with Question Thinking and the Learner and Judger mindset material.

"Since I wasn't there," I said, a bit apprehensively, "maybe you'd suggest ways that you see us employing some of those practices here." The moment those words left my mouth I regretted it. Was I going too far and undercutting my own authority? Was this giving Charles what he wanted?

Meanwhile, he had folded his hands in his lap. His head was slightly bowed as if he was thinking about ways to answer that question. Finally he looked up, drew a deep breath and said, "Every question missed is a potential crisis waiting to happen."

> Every question missed is a potential crisis waiting to happen.

"I'm not sure I understand," I said. "Could you say more?"

"It's one of the things Joseph told us, to emphasize the importance of Question Thinking," Charles said. "He even handed out cards with that sentence printed on it. I've pinned one of those cards to my bulletin board as a reminder."

"I guess maybe our team has been missing a lot of questions about our project," I said. The room went silent. I wasn't sure what to do or say next. All I could think of was that I hadn't until now invited questions from my team. On the contrary, I'd squelched them. I'd been interpreting Charles' questions as criticisms of me. I'd reacted defensively. If Joseph's saying was really true, my reactions had led to a lot of unasked questions. *Was I to blame for my team's lack of participation? What was wrong with me? Why had it taken me so long to see this?* Judger questions tumbled around in my mind. It didn't take a genius to see who was at fault. But I couldn't stop here. If I wanted to move forward and find real solutions, I had to accept what was true and start asking very different kinds of questions—and lots of them. What's more, I had to start encouraging questions from all my team members.

"I need your help," I said. Instantly, I was surprised by the tone of confidence that came through in my voice. "As you know, it's the eleventh hour for our project. If we don't get off the dime and move forward, we're in real trouble."

Charles nodded. "I understand," he said. "And I share your concerns. You have my full pledge that I'm behind you 110 percent."

"That means a lot to me," I said, convinced he was sincere in his pledge. "Let's start with this question: *How do we get past what's been blocking us and our team?*" This was a question I'd come up with in my preparations for this meeting. "In particular, what do *you* need to help us be successful?"

For a moment, Charles seemed taken aback. Then he said, "I'm not sure I have any immediate answers or even the best questions. However, I am sure of one thing—that whatever we're doing in this conversation feels a whole lot better than before. It seems like a good direction." He paused, then added, "I think I've got something that could be helpful to us."

My hackles went up. *Here he goes again*, I thought, reacting like I had a million times before. He's going to challenge my authority. But I quickly stopped myself. In that instant three Self-Q's popped into my mind: *Am I in Judger? How else can I think about this? What do I want to accomplish in this meeting?* If I wanted to clear the air with Charles and get the team moving forward, I had to let go of my old assumptions. Everything depended on it.

"I'm all ears," I said.

"It's something Joseph showed us," Charles said. "He called it Q-Storming."

At that moment you could have knocked me over with a feather. Just a day before I would have done anything to shut Charles down. Today I just said, "Tell me about it."

Charles got up and went over to the flipchart that had become a permanent fixture in my office and picked up a blue felt-tip marker. "The goal," he explained, "is not to come up with answers, ideas, or solutions. Instead we want to come up with as many new *questions* as possible. Just throw out questions as fast as we can, while I write them down."

"In other words, with no responses or discussion in between," I guessed.

"Exactly. Joseph said the goal is to open new doors in our minds . . . behind every door we might find another answer or solution. Every new question just expands our range of possibilities. I think his exact words were 'A question not asked is a door not opened.'

A question not asked is a door not opened.

"You always start by describing the problematic situation and your goals for change," Charles explained. "After that you figure out what assumptions you have about the situation."

"You mean like the assumption I made that you'd have trouble working with me," I said.

Charles cringed but then nodded. "Once you've got your goals and assumptions clarified, you take a look at the actual facts about the situation. After that you start brainstorming new questions. For example, you might ask: *In what ways can we best work together to meet our targets?*" He wrote that question on the flipchart. After that, he immediately added another question: *What do I want to change about the team?*

"What *don't* we want to change!" I exclaimed.

"Joseph says the secret of successful Q-Storming is to stay in Learner and be careful about how you phrase the questions," Charles continued. "If we're to get the results we want, the questions need to be in the first person . . . in other words, asking in terms of *I* or *we.*"

"Okay," I said. "You mean like: *What would I like to see happen that isn't happening now? How can we all listen better? What can I do to be more creative?*"

"Great questions," Charles said, writing as fast as he could and underlining all the *I's* and *we's.*

I'm not sure where it came from, but right after he said this, a new question popped out of my mouth: *How can I keep the communication channels open between you and me and our other team members?*

I thought I saw Charles smile, but he didn't say anything, just wrote my last question on the flipchart. Then he added another of his own: *What will help me to keep asking the right kinds of questions?*

How do we state our goals better, so everybody can be more aligned?

"And inspired?" Charles added.

"Exactly," I said.

"Let's keep going. More questions!" Charles exclaimed. He continued to jot them down on the flipchart, scrawling them out with the blue felt-tip pen:

What kind of fuel can I bring to keep our team running?

How do I keep from being judgmental?

What are the greatest strengths of each team member?"

How do we make sure we follow through on all our promises?

How can I assure each member it's okay to ask for help?

We both fired off questions in rapid succession. I was surprised at how naturally and easily Charles and I were working together. In no time we had four sheets covered with questions, and they were all over the floor. Finally, I suggested we stop and review what we'd done.

Charles stepped back from the flipchart and said, "Joseph explained that it was important to notice if there are any questions we hadn't asked before. The new questions can make the biggest difference."

I quickly looked over the list still on the flipchart and shuffled through the sheets of questions on the floor. "Yes, quite a few," I admitted, frankly startled at how many I really hadn't asked.

Charles and I stood in front of the flipchart and then taped the other sheets up on the wall. We spent the next half hour looking over all our questions and adding new ones here and there. As we began discussing the questions it became clearer to me why we'd been stuck and what would help us make the changes we needed.

Seeing all those questions written down helped me slip into my self-coaching mode and look at my present situation more objectively. Q-Storming allowed me to see possibilities I never would have come up with on my own.

I remembered Alexa's story about her big breakthrough, how changing the kinds of questions she asked had changed the whole company. I was getting an inkling of how that could happen for us as well.

Charles was copying our questions into his tablet for later reference.

I perched on the edge of my desk, staring at the flip-chart. "I think I have a question to add to our list," I said. I went up to the chart, turned to a new sheet and wrote: *What will help each of us make our best contribution?*

"Nice," Charles said, nodding.

That word *contribution* suddenly became the central focus of my attention. In my zeal to assert my old role as the answer man, I had hardly ever asked questions such as: *What do other people have to offer? What do they need and want? What is my effect on them?* I saw even more deeply how the failure of the team, the team I used to call a night-mare, had been the leader of the team: me! I had been the problem all along!

"I think I could spend the next few hours discussing what we've just accomplished here," I said. "But do you know what the most valuable lessons are for me in all of this?"

Charles shook his head.

"First, this was a great demonstration that questions have the power to open things up and maybe even turn things around. I can imagine using Q-Storming with the team—and as soon as possible! Second, I've got a whole new perspective on the ways that questions can help us better appreciate and understand the people around us."

These revelations were opening another very big door for me, with a new question coming into sharp focus: *Am I willing to allow others to help me or contribute to solving our problems?*

"Ben," Charles said. "Before this meeting, I wasn't at all sure I would be able to stay on here at QTec. To tell the truth, working with you had started feeling like it was more trouble than it was worth."

"That painful, huh?" I did my best to cover up how ill at ease his statement made me feel. I even felt the tug of defensiveness. But then something shifted inside me. I felt my face break into an embarrassed grin, then I just laughed out loud. "I sympathize with you entirely," I said.

"Sorry, I guess I came off pretty harsh, didn't I?" Charles said. "But I needed to tell you that."

"Yes, you did," I said. "We both needed that." I extended my hand to him. He hesitated for just a second and then shook it warmly. We had made our peace, and it felt great. In the process I'd made the breakthrough I'd been hoping for—and changing my questions was the pivot that made the difference. I could hardly wait to tell Joseph what had happened.

After Charles left my office, I went back to the flipchart and started blocking out plans for meeting with our team the following morning. This time I wanted to have the right questions to create a Learner environment. That would change everything about the way we worked together. I was sure our results would change because of that. I sat down at my desk, pulled out my notes from my meetings with Joseph and began thumbing through them.

I leaned back in my chair and stared at the little placard on the wall: "Question everything!" Yes, I thought, Joseph was right. It all seemed so simple now. Right. Simple like Einstein's Theory of Relativity!

CHAPTER 11

Amour! Amour!

Out beyond right doing and wrong doing,
there is a field. I'll meet you there.

Rumi

That night, charged up by all that had happened in the meetings with Alexa and Charles, I worked late. In fact, I worked till long after dark, making notes for the meeting the next morning with Charles and the team. I also sent an email to Alexa to check on Joseph's availability for meeting with us within the next few weeks. Time raced by. When I remembered to check the clock it was two hours past the time I told Grace I'd be home. I considered calling but figured she'd be in bed sound asleep, so I decided not to disturb her. On the way home in the car I noticed it was going on eleven o'clock.

When I walked in the house I found Grace sitting alone in the dimly lit living room. She was in her pajamas, reading by a single lamp beside her chair. The moment I greeted her, I knew something was wrong. She silently set aside her book, walked up to me, took my hand, led me over to the sofa and gently told me to sit down. I sat, half expecting her to announce that someone had died—or that she was leaving me. She perched herself on the arm of the overstuffed chair across from me, leaned slightly forward and gazed into my eyes. This was going to be serious.

"Ben," she said, "you have *got* to tell me what's going on with you."

Just as I'd done so many times before, my first instinct was to shrug it off. "I worked late. I told your secretary. . . I considered calling but figured you were asleep."

"It's not about that. You know it isn't." She fixed me with a look that told me she wasn't going to back off.

"There's been a lot of pressure at work. . . deadlines coming up way too fast. . . but I think there was some real progress today. . . nothing to worry about." I knew I was waffling, but to tell the truth I was scared half to death.

Grace shook her head slowly, paused, then asked, "What is it you need right now?"

For a moment I was speechless. Wasn't this the very question I'd asked myself about Charles? *What does the other person need and want?* Was she reading my mind, or had she somehow seen Joseph's *Top 12 Questions for Success*?

"What do I need?" I echoed nervously. "You know, at this point I'm not even sure." I wasn't lying to her. I really didn't know.

"Okay, let me tell you what I've been noticing," Grace began. "Not long after you took this job, our whole relationship changed. You changed. I began to worry it was something about me. Did you suddenly feel that marrying me had been a mistake? Had I done something that offended or hurt you?"

I held up my hand. "Oh, Grace, it isn't anything like that, not at all!" The idea that I had been so oblivious to her feelings made we want to weep.

"That's what I realized after studying the Choice Map," she said. "You know what became clear—we've both been going down the Judger path. I know I've been judging myself and you, and I see you being in Judger, too."

I had been bursting to tell her about my breakthrough with Charles, how it had already changed so much for me at work. Suddenly even that faded into the background. I searched for words to tell Grace how sorry I was to have caused her such pain. But all I could do at first was nod and say I agreed with her.

"I'm filled with questions about us," Grace continued. "But until this afternoon my questions were mostly Judger ones. Then I started looking for things I might do or say to keep us from getting stuck in the Judger Pit."

"This is really hard for me to hear," I said, bowing my head, "I guess there's no easy way to say this. . . no other way through it. . ." I prayed I wasn't going to lose it.

Grace suddenly looked as pale as a ghost. "Please let this not be what I'm thinking," she said, her voice shaky and fearful.

"What?" An alarm went off in my head. All sorts of possibilities raced through my mind. She leaned forward from the arm of her chair, staring at me. I took a deep breath. "Wait," I blurted out. "What *are* you thinking? You don't think. . ."

"It's all the long nights you've spent at the office, all the excuses for not coming home, failing to call even to let me know where you were, not having time for me. . . for *us*." She paused. "What did you expect me to think?"

"Grace. . . I swear, it's nothing like that." This was really tough! It had never occurred to me that she might have interpreted my long hours at work like this.

I shook my head slowly, partly because I couldn't believe what I was hearing and partly to assure her I was not having an affair. "I would never do that, Grace." I paused and gave a lot of thought to what I was going to say next. "There's something I want to tell you that I'm finding very difficult to say. I hope you won't end up hating me for it. . . maybe even as much as if there'd been another woman."

My face felt hot and my voice sounded shaky. I had no idea what Grace's reaction would be in the next few moments. I was afraid that she might even walk out on me when I told her the truth about my failures at work.

"I didn't exactly tell you the truth about Joseph and how I got the Choice Map," I began. "I was in a real jam at work. Things were not going well at all. As I saw it, I had to choose between going to Joseph for executive coaching or handing in my resignation."

"Your resignation! Is that what this is all about? Oh, Ben, I'm so sorry!"

"For months I've been afraid I wasn't cut out to be a leader. Just the opposite! Everything I tried just seemed to get crappy results. I was letting down everyone who'd believed in me, you as well as Alexa. And certainly the team I was supposed to be leading! And if this job didn't work out. . . well, I was afraid of how it would affect us. . . you and me. Frankly, I was afraid you'd think I wasn't good enough for you."

We were both silent for several moments, then she asked quietly, "When did you first realize things weren't working out in the new job?"

"A few weeks into it," I confessed. "At first it was great. I really thought I could handle the leadership thing. Then I was hit with one challenge after another that I couldn't manage, until I felt like I was drowning. . . I just couldn't find the answers."

"Wait," she interrupted. "You've had all of that going on for all this time and you never told me about it?"

"You're angry, Grace, aren't you? I just knew it was going to turn out like this. I'm really sorry. But I think things are turning around for me, in fact, I'm sure of it. . ."

"Wait a second," Grace said. "Back up. You knew *what*? What did you think was going to turn out like this? Do you know why I'm angry at you? Are you sure you know why?"

"Of course I do. For screwing up at this job."

"No! No! No! That's not it at all!" She practically shouted this at me.

"Then for what?" I asked, totally taken aback. Had she found some offense that was even worse, something I didn't even know about yet? I wracked my brain for an explanation.

"What I'm upset about is that you've kept your problems a secret from me. You're my husband, and you didn't let me know about something this important to *both* of us."

"I had every intention of telling you but only after I got things rolling again. I was pretty sure I could get a new job right away, and things would get better and you would never have to know."

"In other words, you were going to continue trying to cover this up and keep me in the dark." Suddenly she looked like she wanted to punch me. "Good grief, Ben, how could you be so clueless?"

I stared back at her like she was a stranger. I really didn't know what to say.

"Listen to me," she said. "You better get what I'm about to say, or we're never going to make it. I *want* you to share what's real with me, your troubles, your doubts, your victories, all of it. I *need* you to. That's such an important part of marriage for me. That's what helps me feel connected. When I'm having trouble at work, I talk it over with you, don't I?"

"Sure. I guess you do. I never thought about it."

"You never thought about it! Are you kidding me? Do you remember what I asked you when you came in tonight?"

"Yes, you asked me what I needed."

"You haven't answered me," she said. "You need to do that. I *want* you to. Right now."

My jaw dropped and I just stared into Grace's eyes for a long time. I don't know how much time passed. Maybe it was just seconds, but those moments are imprinted in my mind forever. *What do you need?* Those four words, asked with so much loving care, were like laser beams cutting through a stone wall I hadn't even known I had erected around me, around my heart.

"What I want. . ." I began, "I guess if I'm being totally honest right now, I want to tell you everything that's been happening to me and not let my fears stop me."

I paused to check out Grace's expression before continuing. She was smiling but there was something else in her face that I couldn't quite read. In spite of that, I had to press on.

"I've had to confront my own limitations," I began, working up my courage. "I've spent way too much time in Judger and have made a lot of assumptions—hurtful ones—about myself as well as other people. All of this has caused major problems at work. And one of the toughest parts I've had to face is that. . . well, there's more to life than being the answer man. I've got a huge amount to learn. At least now I've got some better choices, thanks to our friend Joseph."

At that point, I poured out the whole story of what I'd gone through in the past few months, how I'd been scared to death that if I didn't succeed in this new position, Alexa would conclude that I couldn't make it as a leader at QTec. There had been so many days I'd felt like a loser that I didn't dare admit I was sliding faster and deeper into the Judger Pit. When I got to the end of my story, Grace got up from the arm of the chair where she'd been sitting. She came over and sat down in my lap, enfolding my head in her arms.

"I love you very much," she said. "I love you even more because of all that you've just shared with me. But promise me that you'll never hold out on me again. Promise?"

"It's not going to be easy," I told her. "Habits are hard to break. Besides, at work I've learned that you don't get ahead by whining."

"You're not whining! There's a huge difference between being a crybaby and being honest. We should always be open to asking each other what's going on and feel safe about telling the truth. Remember we're in this together."

There it was again. . . creating room for people to ask questions openly and to listen generously. This conversation was taking the breakthrough I'd had at work to a whole new level. Did I fully understand it all yet? I didn't. But what I did see, quite clearly, was that Joseph's methods worked as well at home as they did at work.

I don't remember the exact words I used though I do remember telling Grace how much this conversation meant to me. I thanked her for asking the questions she had, for listening to my problems, and for putting up with me during a very difficult time.

Grace kissed me gently on the lips. In that instant, I knew something important had changed, not just between Grace and me but in the whole way I looked at the world.

As we headed for the stairs that night, our arms were still around each other, making it difficult to walk. We laughed as we stumbled comically on the first steps. I told her I didn't want to let go but we'd never make it to the top entwined like this.

She smiled playfully, "But we could try!"

We kissed again and I suddenly got serious: "Can I ask you a question?"

"Anytime," Grace said, with a sparkle in her eyes. "Just anytime at all."

CHAPTER 12

The Bottom Line

Creativity is bound up in our ability
to find new ways around old problems.

Martin Seligman

Sitting at my desk this afternoon, I leaned back in my chair and reflected on all we had accomplished at QTec in the recent past. In my right hand I held the rosewood paper-weight Joseph had given me several years ago. Once again I read the words on its sterling silver plaque: *Great results begin with great questions.* Those words and everything I'd learned from Joseph had become my inner compass. Question Thinking had opened up a part of my mind I might never have otherwise discovered, guiding me safely through some pretty rough terrain.

My mind drifted back to that dark day when I drafted my resignation letter, certain I hadn't lived up to Alexa's expectations and believing that she wanted to let me go. I had prepared a careful statement, thanking her for the trust she'd placed in me and acknowledging I wasn't the right person for the job. I just didn't have the leadership skills she was looking for, and I didn't know where to even start developing them. While mentally rehearsing how I would handle the actual meeting with her, Judger questions had filled my mind: *What was wrong with me? What had made me think I could succeed as a leader? How could I tell Grace I had screwed up so badly?*

As you already know, what happened in that meeting with Alexa was quite different from what I'd feared. To my surprise she'd refused to even read my resignation letter. Instead, she had referred me to Joseph for executive coaching. When she described what he did I was skeptical, but Alexa was so enthusiastic I couldn't refuse. She handed me his business card and I instantly spotted that big question mark on it. It nearly leapt off the paper. I hope Alexa didn't notice how I'd rolled my eyes. This guy obviously couldn't be much help to me. I'd built my reputation on being the answer man, and Alexa was recommending somebody specializing in a method called "Question Thinking." No way could that work.

I was in for a big surprise. When I put Joseph's system to the test, it produced excellent results for me. And while it wasn't easy to accept this fact, it soon became clear that that Judger mindset of mine had been jamming up the works for a very long time. The more Judger I was with my team, the more they seemed to resist everything I tried. I think it was soon after this realization that I began communicating with them on purpose from what Joseph calls Learner mindset.

At the same time I started *asking* more and *telling* less. Rather quickly it became apparent that things were turning around for us and we were starting to see the collaborative spirit that characterizes our team today.

By cultivating my Learner mindset, the contentious, adversarial relationship I'd had with Charles changed dramatically. Thanks to the Choice Map and Q-Storming we rather easily navigated beyond the rough waters that had developed between us. And as Charles's and my working relationship got smoother and smoother, the methods we were employing caught on with those around us. Early on I'd believed everyone on my team would have to change before things improved. It turned out that the only person I had to change was me! Charles and my relationship became one of the most productive and innovative collaborations I have ever experienced. One thing was certain, my leadership of our team, and getting our product to market before the competition, couldn't have happened without Joseph's coaching – and without those changes in me.

Some months after our product went to market, Joseph and I met for lunch, and he reminded me of that day I got stuck in traffic and called him up in frustration. He said he had something to share with me about that. He handed me an article on the neuroscience of stress and its implications for executive coaching. I didn't know what this had to do with me, but I had learned that Joseph was full of surprises. The article told about the *amygdalae,* little almond-shaped

masses of cells deep in our brains, one for the left hemi-
sphere of the brain, the other for the right. I looked up at
Joseph quizzically, wondering why I was supposed to read
this. He said that the article might help me further appreciate the power of Question Thinking and the Choice Map
and how they'd helped me make the progress I had.

Joseph sipped his coffee as I started reading the article.
It told how, whenever we experience a threat that makes
us fearful, anything from having a close call in traffic to
the pressure of a tight deadline, the amygdala triggers the
secretion of certain hormones that change our brain chem-
istry and spread throughout our bodies. This is the classic fight-or-flight response. I'd learned that much in high
school biology but not the part about the amygdala. I still
didn't get how this applied to people in leadership.

Long ago, the article said, this tiny mass of cells was
our best defense against saber-toothed tigers, warning us
of danger. Today, these same primitive responses can be
triggered by an upsetting call from the boss or our spouse.
Suddenly we're on high alert, ready to take on any com-
ers—or run like crazy. And because we're civilized people
running or fighting usually aren't great options. We're
stuck with all the chemicals the amygdala has sent out,
we are still feeling the urge to run or fight, and the more
those feelings take over the more uncomfortable we get.
And sometimes those emotions make us freeze up and
feel paralyzed.

Joseph remained quiet, giving me time to read the article. I told him, "It's nice to know that my agitation and frustration in the car that day—to say nothing of my whole body tightening up—wasn't just my imagination. It was all my amygdala's fault!"

Joseph laughed.

"Still," I continued, "you can't deny that the whole thing was compounded by being late for that meeting with Charles, which I was really dreading."

"What was it that changed what you were experiencing that day?" Joseph asked.

"It was those three Switching questions you gave me: *What assumptions am I making? How else can I think about this? What is the other person thinking, feeling, and wanting?* As soon as I began asking them, something shifted inside me. Those Switching questions helped me to get into my Learner mindset. I felt like I'd been released from the grip of all those Judger feelings."

"Where did your focus go at that point?"

"It shifted to Charles, but I was asking very different questions than I had before. I wasn't in Judger about him. Instead, I was consciously asking Learner questions about my own assumptions. And I was feeling much calmer, no longer stuck in that rut about Charles being my nemesis."

"Had anything changed *outside* you? Had the traffic changed? Had the problems you've been facing changed? Had Charles changed?"

"No, nothing outside me had changed. Traffic still wasn't moving. But those questions of yours changed how I was relating to the whole thing. By the time I got to my meeting I was feeling fairly confident that I could have a more productive conversation with Charles. And as you already know, that is exactly what happened. That meeting with him turned out to be a real breakthrough."

Joseph was looking as pleased as I felt.

"When I was beginning this work," he said, "I was particularly interested in how far off the mark our responses can get when we let those primal reactions of the amygdala pull our strings. I guess you could say it's my passion to create tools and methods that give us the capacity of choice with our reactions to the amygdala—though I didn't think of it in those terms at the time. I was thinking mostly in terms of self-management.

"What today I call Question Thinking goes hand in hand with good leadership, fostering environments that are constructive, collaborative, and creative. Through the years one of my greatest rewards has been to witness how these tools and strategies help leaders to develop."

"I can see why you couldn't do all that with the amygdala pulling your strings," I reflected, thinking about what QT had done for me so far, both at work and with Grace.

I glanced at the article Joseph had given me. One line jumped out: "Each time we are hijacked by the amygdala, we end up wasting time and energy that could have gone toward constructive and satisfying solutions." Wasn't this the essence of what Joseph called a Judger hijack? I wondered if Joseph was a friend of the author's. Maybe Joseph himself was the author of the article, writing under a pseudonym.

I looked up from my reading. Joseph took another sip from his cup, set it back on its saucer, and looked across the table at me expectantly.

"I'm beginning to put it together," I said. "Could it be that this work of yours is rewiring my brain? That's the way it feels sometimes." Though I was making a joke, I have to admit that his work really had given me a very different way of thinking. My brain was making vast new connections.

Joseph nodded slowly and smiled, the corners of his eyes crinkling the way they always do when he is pleased. "When I began this work," he said, "I was interested in what it would take for people to get better at managing their inner states. I knew that at the root of our Judger reactions we usually find some kind of fear, even if it doesn't look that way. Fear naturally pushes us toward Judger. It's a facet of our survival instincts to create worst case scenarios so we feel ready for whatever life throws at us."

"That's why you say we're all recovering Judgers," I interjected.

"Yes, yes! That's exactly right. The bottom line is that leaders need to be self-possessed—to have the awareness and skills for self-management regardless of what's going on around them. They need to be able to lead themselves before they can be truly effective at leading others. That's a good description of the process you went through in the car after we spoke that day. You literally changed your internal state, and from there your perceptions and options broadened considerably.

"It's very clear that if leaders allow circumstances and feelings to take them over, they lose their ability to be proactive and strategic. They run the risk of leading with 'ready-fire-aim' behaviors instead of 'ready-aim-fire' ones. They eventually lose the confidence and trust of those around them. . ."

"Which is why asking Switching questions and getting back to Learner mindset is so important," I mused, thinking that this is important for everybody, not just leaders. "Isn't that the real bottom line?"

I guess I drifted off for a second, remembering what Switching questions and the Learner mindset had done for my relationship with Grace. I wanted to share this with Joseph, but he was glancing at his watch and telling me about an appointment he had to keep. He stood up, reached across the table, and shook hands with me, his grip firm and warm.

There was something in that moment of contact that made me realize how much working with him had changed my life. . . and how I'd nearly passed up that opportunity when Alexa first told me about him. I felt embarrassed as I remembered how I'd scoffed at that big question mark on Joseph's card. My whole identity had been tied up with being the Answer Man! Today a question mark means something very different for me: it's a symbol that has become filled with possibilities. . .

———

With a number of successes behind me, I believed I had made my mark at QTec. But I was also aware of new challenges on the horizon. Alexa was developing plans for QTec's further expansion, which was making me nervous. I was happy in my present position and was gaining confidence in my leadership skills. With everything going so well, I didn't want things to change. But every day I heard rumors about Alexa's restructuring of the company. This wasn't news to me, of course. But whenever I'd heard about a company restructuring it usually meant downsizing and people losing their once safe jobs.

Alexa hadn't talked to me about specific roles I might play in the plans that were underway. Would she include me in a larger leadership position? Or had my failures before Joseph's coaching given her second thoughts about me? My shoulders tensed up whenever these questions popped into my mind, signaling me that I was slipping into Judger. I tried to at least stay neutral until I could be surer of the facts.

Then one day, while I was immersed in some reports Charles and I had been working on, the phone rang, jolting me to attention. Alexa's secretary was calling. Was I free to come down to a meeting with the boss in a half-hour or so? And would I please bring that green folder along. I'd know the one. Yes, I knew the one alright. It was the folder with that resignation I'd written. What did Alexa want with that? Hadn't we gotten past that business?

I finished the task I was working on, grabbed the green folder from my desk drawer, and quickly glanced inside. My resignation letter stared back at me. Should I review what I'd written? No! I tucked the folder under my arm and marched down the hall, feeling my belly knotting up. As I stood outside the big double doors of Alexa's office, I heard voices inside. That gave me another twinge of concern. *Echoes of the amygdala!* This time Joseph's words came back to me: "You have choice." Yes. I have choice. Time for my observer self to step up. I took a few deep breaths and steadied myself. "You can handle anything Alexa has in store for you if you stay in Learner," I reminded myself. I raised my hand and tapped lightly on the door.

"Come on in," Alexa called out cheerfully. She opened the door and stood just inside, greeting me with an open, friendly smile that lifted my spirits considerably. Joseph was sitting on one of the two overstuffed sofas separated by the wide coffee table in the meeting area. He stood up as I crossed the room. We exchanged greetings, and I sat down on the sofa across from him. For a second, my eyes were drawn to something on the coffee table. It appeared to be a framed picture turned face down.

"Did you bring the envelope?" Alexa asked, pointing at the green folder.

What envelope was she talking about? I lay the green folder on the coffee table and flipped it open. Only then did I remember the sealed envelope she'd handed me in that meeting when I tried to resign. It had been hidden under my resignation letter.

"This?" I asked, holding up the envelope.

Alexa nodded. "It's time to open it."

Joseph produced a small silver pen knife from his pocket, opened the blade, and held it out to me, handle first. "This must be done with appropriate decorum," he said, in an exaggeratedly ceremonious voice. I could almost imagine drum rolls.

I sliced open the envelope and read Alexa's distinctive handwriting on the note inside: "Ben in Joseph's Hall of Fame." *What did this mean?* And then Joseph was handing me that object I'd noticed on the coffee table moments before. I took it in my hands, admiring the beautifully finished mahogany frame as my eyes scanned the printed document under the glass. I thought it might be an article from *Fortune* or *Forbes*. But no, there was a photo of *me* at the top. Grace must have supplied that picture, since only she knew it was my favorite picture of me.

I looked up and caught Alexa's eye. "When I hired you, Ben," she said, "I knew it was a gamble since you'd never held that kind of leadership position. This was a big unknown. On the other hand, I'd also never seen you back away from a challenge, no matter how big."

"Well, there's always a first time," I said. "Had you not referred me to Joseph, I might have vanished down the highway like the proverbial Road Runner in a whirlwind of dust!"

Alexa laughed. "I doubt that very much. That's just not the way I think of you at all, Ben."

"Nobody's denying that you fumbled," Joseph added. "What impressed me was how you picked yourself up, got your hands on the ball again, and made the run for the winning score."

"Your recovery confirmed my instincts about you," Alexa said. "You see, I subscribe to the belief that failure is often crucial for learning how to do something well. I was quite certain that with Joseph's coaching, you would come out on top."

> Failure is often crucial for learning how to do something well.

She paused, giving me time to look over the document. It was like those other write-ups I'd seen in Joseph's

Question Thinking Hall of Fame, describing how different people had used QT to surmount difficult challenges.
Mine described how I'd led my team to the breakthrough
that helped turn QTec around. Reading it made it clearer
to me how Question Thinking had helped me develop my
own natural leadership abilities. *Not to mention what it
had done for my relationship with Grace,* I thought with a
smile.

As I became more confident with employing Question
Thinking, I'd been pleasantly surprised to see how others around me picked up on it, almost as if by osmosis. Of
course, Charles and I handed out Choice Maps to everyone on our team and posted others throughout our offices.
People frequently asked questions about them. Charles and
I were always glad to talk about the Choice Map. Even after
our explanation a person would linger at the map tracing the
paths with their finger, perhaps considering ways it might
apply in their own life.

As our team put the lessons of the Choice Map into
action, our work environment became increasingly relaxed
and open. When one of us caught ourselves getting negative, we'd usually follow up with a spontaneous, "Sorry,
I guess that was pretty Judger of me." Smiles and laughter
replaced the rather downcast atmosphere of earlier times.
We shared what was on our minds with greater ease and
were much more creative, which naturally made problem
solving and collaboration successful.

We all began asking more questions—Learner questions. These days I smile as I observe people deep in thought,
studying their Choice Maps as they work though problems
or prepare for meetings. I often reflect on something Joseph
once told me: "We live in the worlds our questions create."
How true that is! I have learned to listen in new ways—with
my Learner ears, of course—and to stay on point even when
conflicts threaten, which happens less and less frequently.

Today, my Question Thinking Hall of Fame document
hangs proudly behind my desk. Another copy hangs in the
Hall of Fame gallery in Joseph's office. Seeing it each day
reminds me of the power of Joseph's teachings and how
grateful I am for the huge difference they have made in
my life.

The Inquiring Leader

*Poor leaders rarely ask questions of themselves or others.
Good leaders, on the other hand, ask many questions.
Great leaders ask the great questions.*

Michael Marquardt

One morning Alexa swept into my office waving a printout of an article from *The Wall Street Journal*. She plopped it on my desk, her face lighting up with a big smile. Before I could read the article she explained that a few weeks ago she'd been interviewed by a reporter following a keynote presentation she'd given in Washington, D.C. She had nearly forgotten about it until today when they sent her a prepublication copy for her approval.

The article was titled "Inquiring Leadership: Cultivating High Levels of Engagement, Collaboration, and Innovation in the Workplace." The article's lead line addressed how inquiring leadership had resulted not just in turning QTec around but in producing profits beyond all expectations. My eye went to a paragraph where Alexa had highlighted my name. During the interview Alexa had used me as an example of the kind of leader—what she calls an inquiring leader—that we were developing at QTec. Until then I'd never seen myself as any kind of a model for other people. I barely knew what to say. Before she left my office she called Joseph to share the news with him. Later that afternoon the three of us met over a bottle of Alexa's favorite wine to celebrate the occasion and toast our future.

"This article is a milestone," Joseph said as soon as he finished reading it. " One section especially pops out at me. It's a quote from you, Alexa: 'The culture of any organization is created either by design or by default, and default typically tilts toward the negative and toward Judger. For this reason, it's critically important to build an intentional Learner culture. And this can only happen through intentional Learner leadership.'"

Alexa nodded. "QT's universality—that is, how it guides clearer, more precise thinking and communication—minimizes interpersonal challenges, which ultimately results in greater productivity."

Turning to me Alexa said, "We've had Joseph as an outside consultant focusing mostly on individual coaching and occasional QT workshops. It's time to extend the influence of QT throughout the whole company. As you've seen with your team, QT provides a shared language, with simple, highly intuitive tools and practices."

"That's true," I said. "It seems like people are always pulling out a Choice Map in the middle of a meeting and saying, 'Hey, guys, I think we're heading down the Judger path.' Or maybe, 'Susan's insight is brilliant. It puts us right back on the Learner path.'"

"That's great to hear," Alexa replied. "QT skills have certainly caught fire with individual leaders whom Joseph has been coaching. I can envision a time when everyone in the organization will be familiar with Joseph's work."

"So what's the next step," I asked, trying to hide my impatience. "How do you see me fitting into your plan?"

Alexa took a deep breath. " I'll start by moving Charles into your position. He's been ready for quite a while."

For an instant I found myself pulled toward the Judger path. Was this a joke? Was she really moving Charles up as my replacement? Where did that leave me? Alexa's announcement triggered some negative feelings I used to have about Charles. It took a second to give my Judger mindset a rest.

"I'll want you to coach Charles through the transition," Alexa said, nodding in Joseph's direction. And then, looking me directly in the eye, she said, "As for you, Ben, I'd like you to head up the team that will bring Question Thinking throughout the *whole* company, stateside, internationally, and with our virtual employees. In effect, you'll become our QT ambassador."

"Me. . .? But. . ." I stammered.

Alexa grinned knowingly. "Ben, you know Question Thinking backward and forward. The unique combination of your struggles and ultimate successes gives you exactly the qualifications I want for this leadership position. I want you to shift gears and think much larger than the leadership of your current team."

"This is a lot to take in," I said, adding, "I hope Joseph will be there to back me up."

Alexa laughed. "Yes, you have my guarantee of that. We're working out the details, lining up people for your team who've been particularly enthusiastic about QT. And I've been talking with Joseph about creating a QT curriculum that includes a lively, engaging e-Learning experience based on the Choice Map. I like the idea of individual and collaborative learning online, including social media. We should encourage individuals and teams to share Learner success stories and new ways they've discovered for using the QT tools."

"That's an exciting vision," I told her. However, as I contemplated this promotion, I felt a stab of anxiety. "This is all so new to me. Are you sure I'm ready for this? Where would I even begin?"

Alexa and Joseph exchanged glances. "You can begin by telling your own story," Joseph said. "Be authentic. Leadership is as much about who you are as it is about what you do. Tell people where you started, where you are now, and what a difference QT has made for you personally, for your team, and for the whole company.

> Leadership is as much about who you are as it is about what you do.

"Share your struggles along with your successes. This is a great way to build trust and alliances—Learner Alliances—that motivate others to want to emulate your attitudes and skills. Your effectiveness as a leader will often depend on these Learner Alliances, with trust and mutual respect based on your example, on people knowing you've been there, you've done it, and now you *live* it. You empower each person to think "If he can do it, so can I," a belief made all the more real as people discover that these are practical, learnable skills, not unique traits of a single individual."

"Like the tools you describe in the QT Workbook," I said. "They've been a lifesaver for my team and me."

Alexa nodded enthusiastically. "In today's world we need to be adaptive and resilient, able to move quickly and strategically, and I believe a Learner culture equips us to deliver on that." She paused. " There's a quote by Edgar H. Schein I've always liked. How does it go? 'The only thing of real importance that leaders do is to create and manage culture.'"

"Yes," Joseph added, "There's another part of that quote that is particularly important. Schein cautions us, 'If you do not manage culture, it manages you, and you may not even be aware of the extent to which this is happening.'"

Alexa looked in my direction. "This is an important piece of your assignment," she told me. "You'll have your finger on the pulse of QTec's culture and its impact on everyone who works here. You've graduated from being the answer man, Ben. I'm offering you the leadership positon of being our global QT ambassador."

For the longest time the two of us sat there, eye to eye. Finally I said, "I feel a like the proverbial trailblazer setting off into new territory," I said.

"You're going to discover you know more than you think," Alexa said. "I'm absolutely sure of it."

"And you come equipped with a map!" Joseph grinned, pointing to the Choice Map that just happened to be on Alexa's wall, beautifully framed.

"Right," Alexa said. "You'll have all the resources you'll need. Imagine what we could accomplish if most of us were in Learner most of the time!"

She glanced over at Joseph, who nodded. Then she turned back to me: "What about it, Ben? Any questions?"

"Questions? Oh, you bet. I've got a million of them! I've become a champion of that Einstein quote you've got posted all over the place—*Question everything!*"

The room was silent for a moment, and then all three of us burst out laughing.

"You two are amazing," Joseph said, after we'd quieted down. "Great things are happening around here, for everybody. Creating an intentional Learner culture—what an inspiring vision! I can't help but wonder: *What can QT make possible for all of us, now and into the future?*"

12 Powerful Tools for Leadership, Coaching, and Life

In these pages, you'll find the 12 Question Thinking tools that Joseph introduced to Ben, in approximately the same order as they occur in the story. I've also included page references so you can refer back to see how Ben applied and benefited from each one.

Each tool is an integral facet of the Question Thinking system, so you may notice that the 12 tools overlap as well as complement one another.

Just as with developing any new skill, the more you use these tools, the more proficient you become. Think of this process as similar to what athletes do, practicing and strengthening to be at their best. Using the exercises in this workbook you will be strengthening and refining your Question Thinking muscles.

You may notice as you read through the workbook that the formats of the last two tools—Coaching and Leadership—are somewhat different from the others. The purpose of the last two tools is to summarize and condense the core concepts of the book, mentally imprinting the lessons so they may be easily accessed at any time. Many coaches, leadership development professionals, and other change agents have found that the tools in this workbook are easily integrated with their own unique work.

Here are some ideas for becoming more skillful in using the tools yourself as well as in sharing them with others, especially in the workplace, contributing to the creation of a Learner culture. Many organizations use *Change Your Questions,* including the tools in this workbook, to focus discussion groups on areas such as team collaboration, pro-ductivity, communication, and innovation. It can be helpful to post copies of the Choice Map in offices and conference rooms to serve as reminders and guides.

Time and time again, readers tell me how Question Thinking has made a positive difference throughout their lives—with their closest relationships, their finances, their health, in their athletic endeavors, in weight management, and even with the challenges of raising teenaged chil-dren! Self-help groups, nonprofit groups, book clubs, and church groups also actively use the ideas and principles in *Change Your Questions, Change Your Life* as guidance.

I love hearing from my readers, especially stories about

how Question Thinking has made a difference in their lives—at work as well as in personal relationships. I invite you to join our learning community (www.InquiryInstitute. com) for access to blogs and other resources and to be connected with others as a dynamic and growing Learner alliance.

|||||||||||||||||||||||||||||||||||||||||||||||||||||||||||||||||||||||||||||||||||||||||

The 12 Tools of Question Thinking

Tool 1	Empower Your Observer
Tool 2	Use the Choice Map as a Guide
Tool 3	Put the Power of Questions to Work
Tool 4	Distinguish Learner and Judger Mindsets and Questions
Tool 5	Make Friends with Judger
Tool 6	Question Assumptions
Tool 7	Take Advantage of Switching Questions
Tool 8	Build Learner Teams
Tool 9	Create Breakthroughs with Q-Storming
Tool 10	Ask the Top 12 Questions for Success
Tool 11	Coaching Self and Others
Tool 12	Leadership—The Power of Question Thinking

||||||||||||||||||||||||||||||||||||||||||||||||||||||||||||||||||||||||||||||||||||||||||||||||||

Tool 1: Empower Your Observer

See Chapter 2, "A Challenge Accepted"

Purpose: To cultivate the ability to be still, calm, and present with ourselves and others. This capacity is the foundation of equanimity that helps us to become more present, centered, resourceful, and strategic. The observer self is also the basis for self-reflection and the ability to engage in intentional change.

Discussion: In Chapter 2, Ben begins learning how to stand outside himself and nonjudgmentally witness his thoughts, feelings, and actions. Joseph explains that we all have this observer capacity. It is sometimes experienced as a feeling of watching a movie in which we are one of the actors, or simply witnessing our own actions from a great distance. The more we develop our observer capacity, the more in charge we can be of our thoughts, feelings, and actions— and the less likely we are to be controlled by people and circumstances outside ourselves.

From the position of observer, we gain the ability to simply notice *what is*, somewhat detached from our own thoughts and feelings. We become more able to distinguish between our perceptions and opinions and what's actually happening around us. It is a way of being more "mindful" of the role our own emotions, opinions, or attachments play in how we view the world. Many spiritual and philosophical traditions recognize this observer capacity as a natural ability that is strengthened by practices such as meditation or the ones described here.

Is it ever possible to become 100 percent objective and open to what's true and real? Of course not. But switching into observer mode, to any degree, is an invaluable skill for negotiating change, making decisions, operating effectively under pressure, and relating well to others. From the observer self we are in an ideal position to recognize the kinds of questions we're asking and to switch to Learner questions when we find ourselves on the Judger path.

Here are three simple ways to empower your observer capacity.

Practice 1: The next time your phone rings at home or at work, stay still and just let it ring. In fact, listen to the ringing. As you do, observe your reaction to the ringing, such as your desire to act by rushing to the phone and picking it up or checking the caller ID. Carefully observe what's going through your mind and body, without taking action (that is, answering the phone) or becoming attached to the thoughts and feelings that are triggered by the ringing phone.

If you wish, imagine that your thoughts and feelings are like clouds moving across the sky, and you're simply and calmly watching the shifting scene.

Practice 2: When you get into a challenging situation in which you have an impulse to act, or you have thoughts or feelings you want to express, just step into your observer mode instead. Remind yourself that, just as with the ringing phone, you do not have to "answer" those impulses. You can cultivate patience as you learn to simply observe. Then, when you do take action, you will be more thoughtful, strategic, and mindful.

Practice 3: The next time you're faced with an important choice, or when you notice you've been hijacked by Judger, take a few quiet minutes to be alone. Sit quietly, noting whatever you are thinking, feeling, or wanting at that moment. Promise yourself that regardless of what you observe, it is not yet time for action. Simply observe and note.

In the most expansive sense, the observer is calmly asking a single Self-Q: *What's present now?* As your observer becomes more refined and skillful, you will become better and better at recognizing when you're in Judger and at simply accepting that this is momentarily where you are. It is this moment of "waking up," noting where you are, that grants each of us the liberating power of true choice.

‖‖

Tool 2: Use the Choice Map as a Guide

See Chapter 3, "The Choice Map"

Purpose: To provide a visual summary and guide for noticing one's Learner/Judger mindset as well as the questions, and the future, that each of these might lead to.

Discussion: You can think of the Choice Map as a mindfulness tool. Throughout Ben's story, the Choice Map helps him to become aware of the kinds of questions he's asking—Learner or Judger—and to consider how he might change his questions for the best results. Here are four ways to work with the Choice Map.

Practice 1: Imagine that you are the figure standing at the crossroads on the left side of the Choice Map. Some thought, feeling, or circumstance has just occurred. It might be related to any area of your life, either professional or personal. Experiment by taking each path separately—that is, by asking yourself either Judger or Learner questions about this situation and carefully considering the results each might produce. If you land in Judger, consider what Switching question might allow you to step onto the Switching Lane and return to Learner territory. Looking at the Choice Map, you can simply ask: *Where am I right now? Am I in Judger? Where do I want to be? What is my ultimate goal in this situation? Which path will take me where I want to go?*

Practice 2: You can use the Choice Map to learn from a past situation that didn't work out the way you would have liked. The Choice Map can help you to discover if a Judger hijack might have blocked your success. If so, what lessons can you learn from this? Knowing what you know, how would you handle that same situation?

Practice 3: You can also use the Choice Map to learn from a situation that *did* work. What Learner questions made the difference? How did those questions help you to avoid the Judger Pit? If any Judger was present, what Switching questions might you have used to move onto the Learner path? What lessons can you draw from these observations that benefit you?

Practice 4: Share the Choice Map with others, at work and at home, and you'll gain at least as much as you give. There's a medical school saying: "See one, do one, teach one, and it's yours!" You could, for example, share the Choice Map with a coachee, a team member, or a project group. Many readers also share the Choice Map with family members and friends. This is an ideal way to reinforce Learner relationships and results with people anywhere in your life. Caution: Make sure you're in Learner mindset when you share the Choice Map with others! (Note: Full color downloads of the Choice Map are available for readers at my website: www. InquiryInstitute.com. Use this code for a free download: CYQ3.)

||||||||||||||||||||||||||||||||||||||||||||||||||||||||||||||||||||||||||||||||||||

Tool 3: Put the Power of Questions to Work

See Chapter 2, "A Challenge Accepted"

This tool has two parts: The first (A) has to do with becoming more aware and effective at asking *internal questions* (the ones we ask ourselves); the second (B) has to do with becoming more prolific and effective at asking *interpersonal questions* (those we ask others).

A: INTERNAL QUESTIONS

Purpose: To become more aware of your Self-Qs and to increase the quantity and quality of your internal questions, the ones you ask yourself.

Discussion: Ben starts to change once he realizes that the questions he asks himself—both Learner and Judger—have a huge impact on the results he's able to achieve. He then begins refining his questions by applying the tools in the Question Thinking system.

All our actions are driven by internal questions that we may or may not be aware of asking ourselves. Even an ordinary activity such as getting ready to go on a vacation is driven by questions. For example, think of a time when you were packing for a trip. You went to your closet, your bureau, and your medicine cabinet and asked yourself questions such as: *What climate(s) will we be in? Do I need evening clothes as well as casual ones? What packs well and doesn't wrinkle?* And, *How long will we be gone?* You answered your questions first in your mind by making a decision, followed by *doing* something about it. You selected some items and put them in your suitcase.

As you think about packing for for a trip, notice that you would ask yourself very different questions depending on whether you were going, say, for an African safari or a lovely week in Paris. And what if you arrived at your destination and discovered you'd forgotten something? That just means you forgot to ask yourself about that item when you were packing for your trip.

These two practices for increasing your awareness of Self-Q's are very simple. The first turns your attention to dis-covering how *prevalent* internal questions are in your life. The second focuses on the *types* of questions you ask yourself and the kinds of experiences and results they produce.

Practice 1: When you get up tomorrow morning, do a little personal question research. Note what questions you're asking yourself as you get dressed. Then, from time to time throughout the day, ask yourself what questions might be driving your behavior in that particular situ-ation, both in terms of your own actions and in terms of your interactions with others. It may take some patient observing to recognize those behavior-generating questions, but stay with it until you are able to recognize the influential role that Self-Qs play in your life.

Practice 2: As a second piece of question research, notice your responses to situations that come up throughout the day. Is your first thought a statement (an answer), or is it a question? If your first thought is a statement, experiment with changing it into a question; notice how shifting from a statement to a question changes your mood, actions, or interactions. Notice any correlations between your statements or questions and the kinds of experiences and results they produce.

B: INTERPERSONAL QUESTIONS

Purpose: To become more aware of the questions you ask others and to be mindful of their possible impact. Also, to increase the quantity and quality of the questions you ask.

Discussion: Throughout Ben's story, Joseph helps him to understand the importance of asking questions in order to:

- Gather information

- Create understanding and learning

- Search for and challenge assumptions

- Build, improve, and sustain relationships
- Clarify and confirm listening
- Stimulate creativity and innovation
- Resolve conflicts and create collaboration
- Set goals and create action plans
- Explore, discover, and create new possibilities

Practice 1: Approximately what is the ratio of questions you ask compared to statements you make (your ask/tell ratio)? Do your communications with others involve more telling than asking? In at least one conversation today, practice asking questions much more and telling or advising much less. What do you notice from this experiment?

Practice 2: Recall a time when a particular question made a positive difference in your personal or professional life. It could have been a question you asked yourself or one that someone asked you. What was the question? What was the result? And what was it about the question that made such a difference?

II

Tool 4: Distinguish Learner and Judger Mindsets and Questions

See Chapter 3, "The Choice Map"
for the list of Learner and Judger Questions

See Chapter 6, "Switching Questions"
for the full Learner/Judger Mindset Chart

Purpose: To help us to distinguish between our Learner and Judger mindsets moment by moment and notice how each affects our thinking, actions, relationships, and results.

Discussion: In Chapter 3, Joseph shows Ben how to use the list of Learner/Judger Questions to identify the kinds of questions he's asking and their impact on him, on other people, and on specific situations. As Ben gains greater facility with Question Thinking, Joseph gives him tools to identify Learner and Judger mindsets and relationships.

The following exercise allows you to have an experience similar to Ben's as he refined his ability to recognize intellectual, emotional, and physiological differences between being in Learner and being in Judger. You can either read the questions to yourself or have another person read them to you.

Practice: Look at the Judger column of the Learner/Judger Questions and notice how the questions affect you physically, emotionally, and intellectually. If you're like most people, Judger questions may lead you to feel fearful, deenergized, negative, tense, or even a little "blue." I often do this exercise in workshops. Some people have even reported that they held their breath or got a headache from thinking with Judger questions!

Now it's time to switch to Learner. Take a deep breath, let go of Judger, and then slowly read or listen to the Learner questions on the right side of the chart. Notice how you feel now. Many people report that Learner questions leave them feeling energized, optimistic, open, hopeful, and more relaxed. They feel encouraged to look for solutions and possibilities. As one workshop participant noted, "When I'm looking with Learner eyes, I feel hopeful about the future."

You may discover, as Ben did, how questions associated with these two mindsets put you in distinctly different moods—and that these different moods position you to think, act, and behave quite differently. You may also discover that the world of experience and possibility is different in Learner than it is in Judger.

Explore how one or the other mindset affects how you interact with the people around you. How does Judger mindset—yours or theirs—affect communications with a colleague, spouse, child, or friend? Then ask yourself about the impact of Learner mindset — yours or theirs—in similar situations.

lIIlll

Tool 5: Make Friends with Judger

See Chapter 4, "We're All Recovering Judgers"

Purpose: To become more aware and accepting of Judger mindset in ourselves and others so that you can learn to just be with Judger rather than reacting to it.

Discussion: In Chapter 4, Ben's growing awareness of his Judger mindset causes him to get increasingly frustrated with himself. But Joseph helps him move beyond this seeming double bind by encouraging him to make friends with Judger.

Although it may seem counterintuitive, the more accepting and "friendly" we can be toward Judger—in ourselves and others—the more liberated we become to make the best choices in any situation. Our awareness and acceptance of Judger is so crucial because it strengthens our ability to switch to Learner. It is in Learner that we are most centered, resourceful, strategic, and connected with others.

Engaging in each of the following practices will heighten your non-judgmental awareness of Judger. After you have completed each one, write down your observations and appreciations for the information and freedom that recognizing and accepting Judger has providedfor you.

Practice 1: Keep a journal and jot down times when you catch yourself and/or others in Judger. Include any actual Judger questions you notice yourself asking. You might also include any physical sensations or moods you associate with Judger.

Practice 2: Place a rubber band around your wrist and snap it lightly any time you notice you've been hijacked by Judger. Then, each time you snap the rubber band, smile and congratulate yourself for your increasing awareness of Judger!

Practice 3: Allot a short period in some neutral situation, such as watching TV, to purposefully be as Judger as you possibly can be. For example, you might be openly judgmental or critical of a newscaster's hair style, voice quality, or clothing. This will heighten your awareness of Judger and therefore your ability to choose switching to Learner.

Practice 4: Don't go Judger on Judger! When you recognize that you are being judgmental about your own Judger, or someone else's, just step back and congratulate your observer self for doing its job. That's what gives you the freedom to choose.

Practice 5: Recognize that every time you do these practices you reinforce your observer self and your ability to
operate from Learner. This is one of the many benefits
we accrue simply by noticing and accepting Judger!

III

Tool 6: Question Assumptions

See Chapter 9, "When the Magic Works"

Purpose: To avoid making mistakes and suffering unintended consequences based on false or incomplete information, both in your own thinking and in your interactions with other people at work and at home.

Discussion: You may remember that both Ben and Grace make faulty assumptions about each other and about colleagues. And these faulty assumptions undermine effective communication and creative thinking. Faulty assumptions make it impossible to build or maintain satisfying relationships. In chapter 11, we learn how Ben and Grace resolve the faulty assumptions in their relationship.

To make an assumption is to believe, without necessarily any basis in fact, that something is true. False assumptions can sabotage our efforts to achieve our goals and deepest desires. After bringing to light any blind spots in our assumptions, we gain new insights and creative possibilities that allow us to move forward in more positive ways.

How do you assess the accuracy of your own assumptions so they don't trip you up—resulting in your committing *assumicide*? First access the courage and willingness to notice and examine your assumptions. The habit of asking skillful questions, both of ourselves and others, helps us uncover blind spots and discover valuable new information, perspectives, and possibilities.

Practice: Think of a situation in which you are stuck, frustrated, or where you are seeking change or different results. Use the following list of assumption-busting questions to help you unearth faulty assumptions that might be blocking or hindering your success. For best results, consider each question thoroughly and write down your responses. Often, the act of writing stimulates deeper reflection and discoveries.

- What assumptions am I making about myself?
- What assumptions am I making about others?
- What am I assuming from the past that may not be true now?
- What am I assuming about available resources?
- What am I assuming about what's impossible—or what is possible?

||||||||||||||||||||||||||||||||||||||||||||||||||||||||||||||||||||||||||||||||||||||||||

Tool 7: Take Advantage of Switching Questions

See Chapter 6, "Switching Questions"

For the ABCD formula, see Chapter 7,
"See with New Eyes, Hear with New Ears"

Purpose: To facilitate easier course corrections from the Judger path onto the Learner path.

Discussion: In Chapter 6, Joseph introduces Switching questions, a special kind of Learner question that depends first on being able to observe Judger. Ben learns to ask Switching questions whenever he finds himself in Judger. The Choice Map helps him to remember this shortcut from Judger back to Learner.

Think of Switching questions as "rescue," "turnaround," or "course-correction" questions. They can literally rescue you from Judger experiences or consequences. Switching questions can give you the opportunity not only to choose a new course but sometimes also to make major breakthroughs. Just as with developing any other new ability, the more you use Switching questions the better you get at it.

By their very nature, Switching questions are from-*to* questions, meaning they can carry us *from* Judger *to*

Learner. We all use Switching questions whether we realize it or not; the more aware we are of using them, the more predictably we are able to choose them at will.

The best Switching questions are those that feel most natural and accessible to you. These are the questions you most easily and consistently reach for and use. The more "grooved in" they are, the more effective they will be. The following list of Switching questions includes some contributed by participants in workshops over the years.

- Am I in Judger? (This awareness is always first.)
- Is this what I want to be feeling?
- Is this what I want to be doing?
- Where would I rather be?
- How can I get there?
- Is this working?
- What are the facts?
- How else can I think about this?
- What assumptions am I making?
- What is the other person thinking, feeling, and wanting?
- What humor can I find in this situation?
- What's my choice or decision right now?

I encourage you to add other switching questions as you think of them.

Practice 1: Think of a past situation that was difficult or frustrating for you but that you managed to turn around. Think about what your Switching questions might have been in those situations. Why did they make a difference? When you discover the questions you asked intuitively, you'll be able to use them more intentionally, skillfully, and successfully.

Practice 2: The ABCD Choice Process—Pick a current challenging situation in which you desire a change and follow the ABCD format described in Ben's story in Chapter 7.

‖‖

Tool 8: Build Learner Teams

See Chapter 8, "Learner Teams and Judger Teams"

Purpose: To learn about the benefits of applying Question Thinking and the Learner/Judger distinctions for teams as well as for organizations.

Discussion: In Chapter 8, Joseph uses the Choice Map to explain the difference between Learner teams and Judger teams. Ben realizes that Learner teams are far more effective and high-performing than Judger ones are. He begins to consider ways of turning his Judger team into a Learner one.

The experience of working on teams can be challenging, and people often deal with these difficulties in Judger ways. They might stop listening, try to push their own agenda, or just blame others when things don't work out. They could go Judger on *themselves* by assuming they have nothing to contribute, by shutting down, and/or by not fully engaging. Or they could become overtly demeaning or critical of another person or of others' ideas. Whatever the case, nobody wins. By introducing the notion of Learner teams, each participant can follow guidelines to suspend Judger and simply step into Learner, which has a positive effect on everyone's experience, productivity, and results.

Practice 1: Ask people whether they've ever been on a Judger team. (They usually laugh.) Then ask if they've ever been on a Learner one. Then simply ask them to describe the differences in terms of experience, collaboration, productivity, and results.

Practice 2: Show people the Choice Map and have a conversation about the effects of Learner and Judger mindsets on the success or failure of the team. Include the notions of Judger costs and Judger stand-offs in your conversation. Then introduce the importance of a Learner Alliance and discuss what it would take for your team to create and commit to that.

Practice 3: Ask people on your team to generate guidelines based on the Choice Map about how best to communicate and collaborate during meetings. Do this as a group process, encouraging each person's contribution.

II

Tool 9: Create Breakthroughs with Q-Storming®

See Chapter 10, "Q-Storming to the Rescue!"

Purpose: To empower collaborative, creative, and strategic thinking that can lead to breakthroughs and more successful results.

Discussion: In the story, Ben learns how to do Q-Storming from Charles, and it contributes to a breakthrough for Ben and their team.

Q-Storming is most often used when breakthroughs are sought in decision making, problem solving, strategic planning, and innovation. It provides a Learner structure for collaborative and creative thinking. It is a tool for moving beyond limited thinking and advancing to novel and extraordinary solutions and answers. While Q-Storming is akin to brainstorming, the goal of this Question Thinking practice is to generate as many *questions* as possible. The expectation is that some of the generated questions will provide desired new openings in thinking. Typically, questions open thinking, whereas answers often close thinking down.

Q-Storming is based on three premises: (1) Great results *begin* with great questions; (2) most any problem can be solved with enough *right questions;* and (3) the questions we *ask ourselves* often provide the most fruitful openings for new thinking and possibilities.

Q-Storming is typically done with a group or team, especially when one is exploring ideas and possibilities. It is also used in goal-oriented conversations between two people, for example, in coaching, leadership, management, and sales. Q-Storming can be done in person or *virtually*, say, with a global team or a coaching client in a different geographic location.

The facilitator and the team focus on developing a clear goal and eliciting assumptions about it before the question-generation phase of Q-Storming. Often at the end, action plans are made or revised based on discoveries made during the Q-Storming session.

QUESTION GUIDELINES

- Questions should be first-person singular or plural, using "I" and "we." You want new questions to think with, not necessarily to ask of someone else.

- Generate questions from Learner mindset and avoid Judger.

- Questions are mostly open-ended, not closed ("How can I?" rather than "Can I?") and ("How can we?" rather than "Can you?")

- Invite courageous and provocative questions, as well as "silly" and "dumb" ones.

Note: Q-Storming is a powerful tool for creative think-ing and for bringing together groups or organizations facing complex or challenges issues. Find out more about Q-Storming training and consulting at: www. InquiryInstitute.com.

||||||||||||||||||||||||||||||||||||||||||||||||||||||||||||||||||||||||||||||||||||||

Tool 10: Ask the Top 12 Questions for Success

See Chapter 9, "When the Magic Works"

Purpose: To offer a useful sequence of questions for individuals and teams so that they may think more comprehensively before making a change or embarking on a new direction.

Discussion: When Ben is caught in traffic and distressed about his upcoming meetings with Alexa and Charles, he calls Joseph, who gives him three of the *Top 12 Questions for Success*. Those three questions help to launch Ben into the series of breakthroughs that lead to his being able to apply Question Thinking for greater success and satisfaction in his job and in his relationship with his wife Grace.

The questions on the *Top 12 List* evolved out of my work with coaching clients, teams, and workshop participants over many years. The list can be used in at least three ways:

1. It is a logical sequence of questions to help you think through any situation you might want to change or improve.

2. You might just want to scan the list for questions you're missing.

3. You can turn to it when you're looking for just the right question to emphasize in a particular situation.

The goal is to integrate these questions into your everyday thinking. Then, when a challenge arises, you'll be able to easily recall some of them. Not every question applies to every situation. That's why you'll want to develop a collection of your favorites and work with them on a regular basis. These questions can open and change your mind. This sequence of questions allows you to unveil new choices, options, and possibilities you might otherwise have missed.

Practice: Think of a situation in which you are stuck, frustrated, or want something to change. Within that situation, you can ask the questions on the following list from several perspectives. Ask them of yourself—*What do I want?* Ask them of other people—*What do you want?* Or ask them of those with whom you have an ongoing relationship—*What do we want?* Here's the list:

1. *What do I want?*
2. *What assumptions am I making?*
3. *What am I responsible for?*
4. *How else can I think about this?*
5. *What is the other person thinking, feeling, and wanting?*
6. *What am I missing or avoiding?*
7. *What can I learn . . .*
    —from this person or situation?
    —from this mistake or failure?
    —from this success?
8. *What questions should I ask (myself and/or others?)*

9. *How can I turn this situation into a win-win one?*
10. *What's possible?*
11. *What are my choices?*
12. *What action steps make the most sense?*

Keep this list in a handy place where you can refer to it often. If you ask these questions frequently enough, they'll become a natural part of your thinking. They'll help you to create more satisfying and successful results in your life every day!

||||||||||||||||||||||||||||||||||||||||||||||||||||||||||||||||||||||||||||||||

Tool 11: Coaching Self and Others

Purpose: Coaches know that asking powerful questions of their clients is key to their success. This coaching tool spotlights special features of the QT methodology for coaching. Here we focus on the benefits of teaching the methodology to clients while using that same methodology to guide them through resolving the issues and goals they've presented.

Discussion: Simultaneously teaching the QT methodology to clients while guiding them through the issues and goals they've presented is an integral part of Question Thinking for coaching. As the client becomes increasingly skillful with these tools, and begins to experience their benefits first hand, the relationship between client and coach becomes increasingly egalitarian and collaborative. Through their shared knowledge of QT, coach and client are able to "speak the same language." As with any coaching relationship, the message at the heart of QT-driven coaching is that the coach will not "fix" the client or the issue; instead, as clients develop skills with the tools and methods of QT they are better equipped to resolve issues and accomplish goals on their own. The coach provides the safe environment where clients gain practical experience with QT while applying it to their own issues and goals.

What clients learn in these coaching sessions makes a

difference for outcomes in their current situation even as they are gaining skills for the future, to self-coach and be more effective at whatever they do. This extends to the client's greater effectiveness with other people both inside and outside the working environment.

Ben's story, throughout the book, illustrates how this process unfolds in a variety of life situations. Early in Ben's first coaching session (Chapter 2) Joseph tells him about the QT methodology they will be using in their work together. Joseph describes it as "a system of skills and tools using questions to expand your approach to any situation." He tells Ben that the tools he'll be learning create a foundation for making wiser choices, asking more and better questions, and getting better results in everything he does. By introducing the methodology in this way Joseph alerts Ben to the fact that his learning the methodology is an integral part of the work they'll be doing together.

Joseph goes on to share with Ben some of the theory behind this work and then presents the first tool: "Empower Your Observer." He gives Ben a workbook that contains short instructions for the tools they will be working with— which is the workbook you are now reading. Each of the 12 tools includes practices for strengthening one's skills.

How you introduce clients to the process described above is important. In the beginning of a coaching engagement, along with developing a trusting relationship and helping clients to articulate their goals, I introduce Question

Thinking and the Choice Map. I explain that I've found that these tools and methods help people to better understand what's been getting in the way of accomplishing their goals. The same tools serve as guides for developing skills for moving beyond any present limitations.

The language and concepts of QT are easily integrated into ongoing conversations with clients. You have probably already noticed how the Choice Map can help you to orient clients in terms of where they are in the Learner-Judger spectrum; for example, when clients have a Choice Map in front of them—especially important in phone or other electronic communication—the coach can ask, "Where would you locate yourself on the Choice Map right now? Are you in Judger? Are you in Learner? Are you in the Judger Pit?" A quick glance at the Choice Map, where these mindsets are graphically expressed, is instructive for both coach and coachee.

Learning Question Thinking is enhanced and accelerated whenever the client is able to immediately experience its benefits first-hand. And as the client's experience and skill with QT grows, so also does the collaborative nature of the coaching sessions grow and deepen.

As clients become more self-aware and skillful at self-management and self-coaching, they are also gaining skill and confidence for building more effective relationships with colleagues and teams outside the coaching relationship. Clients frequently report on how simple it can be to introduce others to QT. As an example, the following note, which came from a coach who'd attended one of my workshops, demonstrates how quickly people can catch on to using the Choice Map:

> I was with some friends at a restaurant and one of them expressed concern about her relationship with her daughter and how they were always arguing. I pulled out a copy of the Choice Map that I carry in my purse and we began looking at ways it might help her. She studied it for a moment and suddenly her eyes lit up and she exclaimed, "I've been in Judger with my daughter!" She immediately started reflecting on ways her Judger mindset had triggered her daughter's defensiveness and anger. Then we talked about Switching questions and she said, "This is like a huge weight lifted from my shoulders." Later, as we got ready to leave she pointed to my Choice Map and asked shyly, "May I keep this?"

Oftentimes, people with no previous exposure to the Choice Map respond to it by saying, "This just makes perfect sense!" For anyone already familiar with Question Thinking, the Choice Map quickly becomes a powerful organizing image for understanding, retaining, and applying the entire methodology. As a client recently told me, "The image of the Choice Map is like a mental magnet that helps me recall everything you've taught me." The map provides coach and client with a shared vocabulary for working together, while at the same time empowering clients with a highly effective self-coaching tool they can use on an ongoing basis.

Practice 1: Recall a past coaching session, before you learned about QT, when you were less than satisfied with the outcome. Perhaps you have found yourself replaying that session in your mind, thinking you should've, could've, would've done it better . . . if only. Now imagine that you are redoing that session, this time introducing the Choice Map to help your client to articulate what might have been getting in his way and to better understand where he and others might have been coming from in their problematic situation. How do you think introducing the Choice Map might have made a difference in the success of that session?

Practice 2: It's good to keep in mind that even the most experienced coaches can go Judger—yes, even about their clients. In Chapter 3, Joseph demonstrated this when he told Ben the story about his superintendent client, when he caught himself in Judger and switched into Learner. Later, in Chapter 8, Joseph tells Ben about a saying of Alexa's: "Learner begets Learner. And Judger begets Judger." This is a good reminder of how important it is to be in Learner when sharing the Choice Map and using QT in general. As Joseph tells Ben in Chapter 3, "No one can help anyone else from a Judger place."

This practice is an opportunity to reinforce your own Learner mindset by checking in with yourself whenever you are in a coaching session or otherwise sharing the Choice Map. You may discover you have some Judger going on with whomever you're speaking to—whether it's a client, a friend, a colleague, or a family member. On rare occasions, I've seen people share the Choice Map in a subtle Judger way, aiming to show how the other person is wrong and is in Judger. If this ever happens to you, it's time to reset yourself to Learner or postpone sharing the Choice Map or talking about the mindset work until you can do so from a Learner place.

In Chapter 5, Kitchen Talk, we have an example of this resetting process. Ben has nervously posted the Choice Map on the refrigerator at Joseph's suggestion. As he and his wife Grace discuss it the next morning, there are a number of times when Ben catches himself in Judger and needs to manage his own mindset to stay in Learner. He uses what he has learned from Joseph and coaches himself: Don't go there, buddy. Then he takes a deep breath, shrugs his shoulders, and recovers himself.

As you get ready to share the Choice Map with another person, consider where you would locate yourself on the map just then. If you discover some Judger you could ask yourself: Why am I in Judger? What Switching questions could I ask myself to move into Learner? What are my goals in sharing the Choice Map with this person?

Use this exercise to explore strategies for staying in Learner throughout any conversation or session, whether it's with a colleague, friend, family member, or client.

|||||||||||||||||||||||||||||||||||||||||||||||||||||||||||||||||||||||||||||||||||||||

Tool 12: Leadership—The Power of Question Thinking

Purpose: To spotlight special contributions of the QT methodology for leadership development, focusing on the methods, benefits, and outcomes of developing as an inquiring leader.

Discussion: In today's business and organizational life there is increasing awareness of the need for leaders who possess highly developed self-management and social skills. Daniel Goleman, author of *Emotional Intelligence*, stated that as we become focused more and more on intellectual and knowledge-based services, people skills become "ever more important, in teamwork, in cooperation, in helping people learn together how to work more effectively." David Rock reflected in *Fortune* magazine: "The ability to work well with other people in a group depends on our ability to appreciate other individuals' emotions. A boss who knows what his staff members really want and care about will be able to design a better team environment than one who is simply focused on the elements of a project."

Throughout *Change Your Questions*, Alexa, Joseph, and eventually Ben represent a composite of the virtues, qualities, and behaviors of what I've termed Inquiring

Leadership. These abilities include being open-minded and curious as well as decisive. Inquiring Leaders are self-aware, self-reflecting, and committed to continuous development, both for themselves and for those around them. They are adaptive, creative, and comfortable with "not knowing" and with not having all the answers. They think, collaborate, and lead strategically, advancing "ready-aim-fire" thinking and behaviors while avoiding "ready-fire-aim" ones. And of course, they intentionally ask many questions of themselves and others.

Following the tenets of good coaching, inquiring leaders understand that asking questions and listening deeply make them smarter and more connected while simultaneously empowering those around them. They use Learner questions to produce powerful results both in their own thinking and decision making, and in communicating with others. They recognize the dangers and missed opportunities of not asking important questions. And they know when to stop questioning and take action!

Inquiring leaders create what I call an intentional Learner culture where inquiry is highly valued and encouraged; they model and mandate inquiry practices throughout their organization. They *ask* more and *tell* and *advise* less, thus inviting collaboration, creative thinking, and new possibilities. Their own words, actions, and behavior invite and encourage engagement, motivation, and commitment, promoting and inspiring trust, respect, and loyalty. In the

Epilogue, this is the Learner culture that Alexa, Joseph, and Ben are envisioning for the future of QTec.

As simple as it may sound, the primary goal of this book is to provide ways for readers to build their self-awareness, self-management, and inquiry skills. QT helps us to become aware of our own Judger mindsets, to become adept at asking ourselves Switching questions, and to cultivate the skills to continually reset ourselves to Learner mindset. These self-management skills, illustrated by the Choice Map, are the heartbeat of inquiring leadership. The QT tools offer a way to *be in training*, getting better and better at building our ability to shift into Learner on purpose, and to grow our personal strength and competence. Using these tools leads to increased self-confidence, relaxed self-control, emotional dexterity, and the ability to be present and effectively responsive to people and circumstances—which is how inquiring leaders create a sustainable Learner culture.

Practice 1: Through using the tools and methods of Question Thinking, we learn to manage difficult situations and emotions, sometimes born of assumptions we've made. We develop a realization that Judger thinking cannot lead to effective leadership, either of ourselves or of others. You can practice this leadership training any time you wish. It's as simple as recalling a leadership situation where your Judger prevented you from being as effective as you would have liked.

As you recall this past experience, trace what occurred on the Choice Map, from the moment it started to the eventual resolution or end. What were the first signals that you might associate with an amygdala hijack, or what I've called a Judger hijack? Perhaps dry mouth, a tightening of the shoulders, back, legs and arms? Maybe you were aware of your heart beating, or you simply felt a certain jolt that you associate with having your buttons pushed. How quickly did you snap back with a counterdefense, moving down the Judger path as you did? Or maybe you suddenly found yourself in the Judger Pit, turning your Judger questions on yourself or on others.

As you are remembering this past leadership experience, recall that the power of QT is in your questions and in your mindset, and in your ability to change the questions that are driving your thinking, feeling, and behaviors. As a coaching client commented: "Judger to Learner—I swear, when the pressure is on I can go back and forth between the two several times a minute. Question Thinking has made it possible for me to stand outside myself and watch it happen. . . . The Switching Lane—that's where the action is, knowing what questions to ask to get back to Learner mindset."

This practice gives you an opportunity for a "do-over." As you think about that leadership situation, look at the Choice Map and speculate about what Switching questions might have made a difference for you at the time. This is very much like what you practiced with Tool #11, except this time the context is a leadership situation. As you move along the Switching Lane, led by your Switching questions, note any changes you are experiencing—whether these changes are physical, intellectual, or emotional.

As you merge onto the Learner path, what changes are you now experiencing? Are you more relaxed and breathing more easily? Are you beginning to think more lucidly and expansively? Maybe you even feel like you are more in charge, like you're leading yourself instead of feeling like a victim of the person or situation that pushed your buttons.

Practice 2: You could also use the Choice Map and this practice to learn from a positive past leadership situation, large or small, that you are pleased about. What Learner questions contributed to your success? Remember that learning is equally valuable whether it comes from successes or failures.

In the days to come, look for opportunities where you can apply what you have discovered in this book. Remember that leaders lead by example and also by empowering others. Whether or not you're in a formal leadership position, you'll always find areas of your life where you'll encounter the challenges of leadership, be they in your family, with friends, or in virtually any social situation—but most important in leading yourself.

END NOTES AND REFERENCES

Foreword: David Wolfskehl is the reader whose successful application of the principles of Question Thinking was described in *Inc. Magazine.* See Leigh Buchanan, "In Praise of Selflessness," *Inc. Magazine* (May 2007).

Introduction: This quote about my work is from *Coaching with the Brain in Mind: Foundations for Practice* by David Rock and Linda J. Page, p. 153 (John Wiley & Sons, Inc. Hoboken, NJ, 2009).

Introduction: Wharton@Work Newsletter of Wharton Business School at the University of Pennsylvania (August 2012), *Nano Tools for Leaders®* "Shifting Mindsets: Questions That Lead to Results."

Introduction: My textbook in cognitive-behavioral psychology, *The Art of the Question: A Guide to Short-Term Question-Centered Therapy,* was published by John Wiley & Sons in 1998 under my maiden name, Marilee Goldberg.

Chapter 2: The example of questions that drove the behavior of nomads was ascribed to psychologist Mark Brown by Michael J. Gelb in *How to Think Like Leonardo da Vinci: Seven Steps to Genius Every Day* (Dell Publications, New York, 2004).

Chapter 6: This quote is from *Man's Search for Meaning* by Viktor E. Frankl, Beacon Press, 2006. Originally published in Austria in 1946 as . . . *trotzdem ja zum Leben sagen: Ein Psychologe erlebt das Konzentrationslager* (which translates as . . . *In Spite of It all, Say Yes to Life: A Psychologist Experiences the Concentration Camp*). The English translation was first published by Beacon Press in 1959.

Chapter 8: Joseph Campbell's story of the farmer and the quote "Where you stumble, there your treasure is" comes from *An Open Life: Joseph Campbell in Conversation with Michael Toms,* selected and edited by John M. Maher and Dennie Briggs (Perennial Library, New York, 1990).

Chapter 8: This article describes research on the relationship between advocacy and inquiry on team performance. Frederickson L. Barbara and Marcial F. Losada, "Positive Affect and the Complex Dynamics of Human Flourishing," *The American Psychologist* (October 2005), 678–686.

Chapter 9: The example about the effect on basketball teams of viewing videos of their successful moves in contrast to their mistakes is from D. Kirschenbaum, "Self-Regulation & Sport Psychology: Nurturing an Emerging Symbiosis," *Journal of Sport Psychology* (1984), 8, 26–34.

Chapter 12: The concept that that "we live in worlds our questions create" relates to the Constructionist Principle of Appreciative Inquiry. See David L. Cooperrider, Frank Barrett, and Suresh Srivastva, "Social Construction and Appreciative Inquiry: A Journey in Organizational Theory," in *Management and Organization: Relational Alternatives to Individualism,* edited by Dian-Marie Hosking, H. Peter Dachler, and Kenneth J. Gergen (Avebury, Aldershot, 1995).

Epilogue: Edgar H. Schein, *Organizational Culture and Leadership,* (Jossey-Bass, San Francisco 2010).

Tool 12: Daniel Goleman, *Emotional Intelligence: Why It Can Matter More Than IQ* (Bantam Books, New York, 1995).

Tool 12: David Rock, "Why Organizations Fail," *Fortune.com* (October 23, 2013).

ACKNOWLEDGMENTS

Writing the third edition of *Change Your Questions, Change Your Life* has provided a gratifying and generative opportunity. There are many to whom I am deeply grateful.

Hal Zina Bennett again brought his editorial brilliance and collaborative generosity to my writing. The spirit and possibility of inquiry are animated by his expertise. My appreciation for his contribution is beyond words.

The Inquiry Institute home team continues to provide an invaluable foundation of friendship, support, and expertise. With Kim Aubry, our Executive Director, as the cornerstone and Anna Barrett as Director of Learning as well as being on our Board of Advisors, I am also grateful to the others on our Board: Walter K. Booker, Scott DiGiammarino, David Goldsmith, Mark Miani, Jeremy Seligman, and Harold Weinstein.

I am grateful to the professionals who support the Inquiry Institute and our work in the world: Terri Andrews, Lina Avallone, Janet Cho, Susan Critelli, Denise Eaton, Eleanor Guare, G. Shawn Hunter, Becky Robinson, Ron Sherman, Marina Sinclair, and Carla Van Dyk. I again thank Diane Chew for the title and Stewart Levine for introducing me to Berrett-Koehler.

Berrett-Koehler exemplifies "publisher as partner," and all BK authors and readers are the beneficiaries. I am most appreciative to their visionary founder and publisher, Steve Piersanti, as well as to Maria Jesús Aguilo, Charlotte Ashlock, Shabnam Banerjee-McFarland, Marina Cook, Michael Crowley, Kristen Frantz, David Marshall, Stacey C. Sawyer, Courtney Schonfeld, and Jeevan Sivasubramaniam. It has been a special pleasure to work again with Detta Penna, the inimitable designer of everything between the covers of this book.

Robert Kramer assigned *Change Your Questions, Change Your Life* to his students at American University's Key Executive Leadership Program in the School of Public Affairs. Little could he have known that that would change *my* life. Eventually I was tapped as an adjunct professor in that program, which for years has been a stimulating environment in which to grow my work on inquiring leadership and learn from fellow faculty members and students. Resounding thanks to Robert as well as Sophie Idilbi, Patrick Malone, Robert Tobias, Ruth Zaplin, and Don Zauderer.

Each of these—friends, family, and colleagues—has also contributed generously to me and my work. I am grateful to you all: Rose and Edward J. Adams, Des Black, Val Cambre, Kathy Carmean, Carol Cartaino, Eric Cheong, Ira Cohen, Lisa Devenish, Ellen Duffield, Kylah Frazier, LeRoy and Selma Crockin Goldberg, Carmella Granado, Walter Haake, Robert Hall, Jim Harrison, Melinda Harrison, Stephanie Harrison,

Popsy Kanagaratnam, Kanu Kogod, Landmark Worldwide, Michael Leech, Kathy Leech, Mark Levy, John McAuley, Elianne Obadia, Linda J. Page, Stephanie Parker, Ellyn Phillips, Brad Pressman, Gemma Qin, Babak Rajaee, Marcia Reynolds, Shana Ring, Ellen Neiley Ritter, Cynda Rushton, Marthine Satris, Cynthia Sexton, Michele Shay, Melinda Sinclair, Lindsay Burr Singla, Henry Toi, Gen Kelsang Wangden, Patrick Williams, and Jim Wilson.

As always, those whom I learn from the most are my students and clients. Inquiry Institute's Chief Question Officer® Certificate Program and our QT workshops bring us students who become our teachers. They come from all over the United States as well as many other countries, including Brazil, Canada, China, Norway, Singapore, and Taiwan. I thank you all.

I am appreciative of Inquiry Institute's global partners, the Leadership Studio at Muskoka Woods—an Inquiry Institute Center of Excellence—in Ontario, Canada, as well as the Brain Capital Group, and Nurture Craft in Singapore.

I am blessed to travel through this life with Ed Adams, my husband and most ardent and stalwart supporter. He brings creativity, wisdom, and fun into our lives every day.

Marilee Adams, Ph.D. Marilee's passion for the transformative power of inquiry has earned her the title of Chief Question Officer. Her work is considered the gold standard for excellence in inquiry in the coaching profession and is widely used for leadership and organizational development. As President/CEO of the Inquiry Institute and the originator of the Question Thinking (QT) methodologies, Marilee is a thought leader, consultant, executive coach, coach trainer, and professional speaker in the United States, Europe, and Asia. She is an adjunct professor at American University's Key Executive Leadership Program in the School of Public Affairs, and is a faculty member at the Institute for Life Coach Training, Adler International Learning, Expedition Coaching, and is a coach for the Society for Organizational Learning.

Question Thinking is known for transforming the "spirit of inquiry" into practical and powerful questioning and thinking skills and tools that make a difference throughout the world. In her coaching and consulting practice, Marilee has witnessed the benefits of QT-based change work for individuals, leaders, teams, organizations, and communities. Some of these organizations include

Areva, Booz Allen, Brother Interntional, DHL, Deluxe, Johnson & Johnson, Lockheed Martin, and Precyse. In government, these include the Brookings Institution, NASA Goddard, the National Defense University, and the Social Security Administration. Professional associations include the Association for Talent Development, the International Coach Federation, Organizational Development Network, and the Society for Human Resource Management.

In the world of coaching, *Change Your Questions* is required or recommended reading in many coach training institutes. Many coaches actively use the book in their coaching engagements, and it used by companies that aim to develop more of a coaching culture.

In the world of education, Marilee has spoken to leaders or has consulted at universities including Columbia, Georgetown McDonough School of Business, Harvard, Princeton, Kansas State, Northern Kentucky University, and Southern Methodist University. She also teaches in the Leadership Institute at Kent State, where Question Thinking is integral to this award winning program. She is on the Advisory Board of Learning Forward New Jersey and consults with public and charter schools including Achievement First.

In the world of healthcare, Marilee has consulted with or spoken at hospitals, including Christiana Care, Hamilton Health Services, Johns Hopkins, MedStar Research Institute, Sunnybrook Hospital, and Toronto General Hospital.

Marilee's first book, *The Art of the Question: A Guide to Short-Term Question-Centered Therapy* (John Wiley & Sons, 1998) was lauded as a "seminal and breakthrough contribution to the field of psychotherapy." The second edition of *Change Your Questions, Change Your Life* was a #1 Amazon Bestseller in Business and Organizational Learning. *Teaching That Changes Lives: 12 Mindset Tools for Igniting the Love of Learning* (Berrett-Koehler, 2013) brought Question Thinking and Marilee's love of inquiry into the world of education. It won a Gold Medal IPPY Publishers Award.

Marilee has coauthored chapters integrating Question Thinking with Appreciative Inquiry as well as with Action Learning. She has also published articles on the expert use of questions in coaching, business, relationships, and organizational transformation. She earned her Ph.D. in Clinical Psychology from the Fielding Graduate Institute and her M.S.W. from Virginia Commonwealth University.

Marilee and her husband, artist and psychologist Ed Adams, live in the river town and arts community of Lambertville, New Jersey. She would love to hear from you at Marilee.Adams@InquiryInstitute.com.

ABOUT THE INQUIRY INSTITUTE

Leadership, engagement, communication, and collaboration are uniquely empowered by the Question Thinking® system of tools and practices pioneered by Marilee Adams and the Inquiry Institute. Our team of coaches, facilitators, and consultants are experts at customizing QT approaches so that individuals, teams, and organizations become more successful and satisfied in realizing their desired results.

Visit our website to explore free resources and become part of our active learning community. You can also learn about Question Thinking-based services and products including:

- QT-based consulting for teams and organizations
- QT-based coach training as well as executive, team, and life coaching
- QT-based public and inhouse workshops, including those based on the Choice Map, Learner/Judger mindsets, and Q-Storming (in person and virtual)
- QT products and resources, including our e-Learning program, *e-Learning: Question Thinking: A Mindful and Practical Approach to Learning, Living, and Change* (based on the Choice Map and Learner/Judger mindsets)
- QT licensing agreements
- Chief Question Officer® Certificate Training Program

Marilee Adams is available for keynote presentations, consulting, and workshops (onsite and virtual), coach training, and executive coaching as well as Q-Storming® training, clinics, and workdays.

Inquiry Institute

www.InquiryInstitute.com
Choice@InquiryInstitute.com
800-250-7823
10 York Street, P.O Box 339
Lambertville, New Jersey 08530-3204

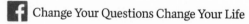 **Inquiry Institute**

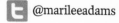 Change Your Questions Change Your Life

@marileeadams

Berrett–Koehler
Publishers

Berrett-Koehler is an independent publisher dedicated to an ambitious mission: *connecting people and ideas to create a world that works for all*.

We believe that to truly create a better world, action is needed at all levels—individual, organizational, and societal. At the individual level, our publications help people align their lives with their values and with their aspirations for a better world. At the organizational level, our publications promote progressive leadership and management practices, socially responsible approaches to business, and humane and effective organizations. At the societal level, our publications advance social and economic justice, shared prosperity, sustainability, and new solutions to national and global issues.

A major theme of our publications is "Opening Up New Space." Berrett-Koehler titles challenge conventional thinking, introduce new ideas, and foster positive change. Their common quest is changing the underlying beliefs, mindsets, institutions, and structures that keep generating the same cycles of problems, no matter who our leaders are or what improvement programs we adopt.

We strive to practice what we preach—to operate our publishing company in line with the ideas in our books. At the core of our approach is stewardship, which we define as a deep sense of responsibility to administer the company for the benefit of all of our "stakeholder" groups: authors, customers, employees, investors, service providers, and the communities and environment around us.

We are grateful to the thousands of readers, authors, and other friends of the company who consider themselves to be part of the "BK Community." We hope that you, too, will join us in our mission.

A BK Life Book

This book is part of our BK Life series. BK Life books change people's lives. They help individuals improve their lives in ways that are beneficial for the families, organizations, communities, nations, and world in which they live and work. To find out more, visit **www.bk-life.com**.

Berrett–Koehler
Publishers

Connecting people and ideas
to create a world that works for all

Dear Reader,

Thank you for picking up this book and joining our worldwide community of Berrett-Koehler readers. We share ideas that bring positive change into people's lives, organizations, and society.

To welcome you, we'd like to offer you a free e-book. You can pick from among twelve of our bestselling books by entering the promotional code **BKP92E** here: http://www.bkconnection.com/welcome.

When you claim your free e-book, we'll also send you a copy of our e-newsletter, the *BK Communiqué*. Although you're free to unsubscribe, there are many benefits to sticking around. In every issue of our newsletter you'll find

- A free e-book
- Tips from famous authors
- Discounts on spotlight titles
- Hilarious insider publishing news
- A chance to win a prize for answering a riddle

Best of all, our readers tell us, "Your newsletter is the only one I actually read." So claim your gift today, and please stay in touch!

Sincerely,

Charlotte Ashlock
Steward of the BK Website

Questions? Comments? Contact me at bkcommunity@bkpub.com.

Certified

Corporation™
bcorporation.net